D1594001

Powerful Premise

Writing the Irresistible

Powerful Premise: Writing the Irresistible
First Edition
Copyright © 2015 William Bernhardt Writing Programs
Red Sneaker Press
An imprint of Babylon Books

All rights reserved

ISBN: 978-0-6924251-0-7

Powerful Premise

Writing the Irresistible

William Bernhardt

The Red Sneaker Writer Series

Other Books by William Bernhardt

Red Sneaker Writer Series

Story Structure: The Key to Successful Fiction
Creating Character: Bringing Your Story to Life
Perfecting Plot: Charting the Hero's Journey
Dynamic Dialogue: Letting Your Story Speak
Sizzling Style: Every Word Matters

The Ben Kincaid Series

Primary Justice
Blind Justice
Deadly Justice
Perfect Justice
Cruel Justice
Naked Justice
Extreme Justice
Dark Justice
Silent Justice

Murder One
Criminal Intent
Hate Crime
Death Row
Capitol Murder
Capitol Threat
Capitol Conspiracy
Capitol Offense
Capitol Betrayal

Other Novels

The Game Master
Nemesis: The Final Case of
Eliot Ness
Dark Eye
The Code of Buddyhood

The Midnight Before
Christmas
Final Round
Double Jeopardy
Strip Search

Poetry

The White Bird

For Young Readers

Equal Justice: The Courage of Ada Lois Sipuel (biography)
Princess Alice and the Dreadful Dragon (illus. by Kerry McGhee)
The Black Sentry
Shine

Edited by William Bernhardt

Legal Briefs

Natural Suspect

Dedicated to all the Red Sneaker Writers:
You can't fail unless you quit.

Why shouldn't truth be stranger than fiction? Fiction, after all, has to make sense.

Mark Twain

TABLE OF CONTENTS

Introduction... i

Chapter One: Defining Premise...........................1

Chapter Two: Something Old, Something New......... 15

Chapter Three: Raising the Stakes...................... 25

Chapter Four: Emotional Appeal........................ 35

Chapter Five: Readily Recognizable Conflict.......... 47

Chapter Six: If You Only Believe........................ 63

Chapter Seven: Pitching................................... 73

Appendix A: Premise Worksheet......................... i

Appendix B: Pitching Dos and Don'ts.................. v

Appendix C: Synopsis..................................... vii

Appendix D: Showing vs. Telling........................ xi

Appendix E: The Writer's Calendar.................... xiii

Appendix F: Commonly Confused Words........... xvii

Appendix G: The Writer's Reading List.............. xxvii

INTRODUCTION

Welcome to the Red Sneaker Writers Book series. If you've read other Red Sneaker publications or attended Red Sneaker events, you can skip to Chapter One. If you're new, let me take a moment to explain.

I've been telling stories for many years, doing almost every kind of writing imaginable. I've been speaking at workshops and conferences almost as long. Every time I step behind the podium I see the same tableau staring back at me: long rows of talented people, most of whom have attended many of these events but are still frustrated by the fact that they haven't sold any books. Yes, the market is tough and agents are hard to find and self-publishing can be frustrating. But when aspiring writers work hard, put it out there, but still don't succeed...there's usually a reason. Too often enormous potential is lost due to a lack of fundamental knowledge. Sometimes a little guidance is all that stands between an unknown writer and a satisfying writing career.

The conference-lecture format is not always the most conducive to writing instruction. And sometimes the teaching I've heard offered is dubious. Too often speakers seem more interested in appearing literary than in providing useful information. Sometimes I feel presenters do more to obfuscate the subject than to explain it, that they want to make writing as mysterious and incomprehensible as possible, either because they think that makes them sound profound or because they don't understand the subject well themselves. How is that going to help anyone?

After giving this some thought, I formulated the Red Sneaker Writing Center. Why Red Sneakers? Because I love my red sneakers. They're practical, flexible, sturdy—and bursting with style and flair. In other words, exactly what writing instruction should be. Practical, flexible, resilient, dynamic, and designed to unleash the creative spirit, to give the imagination a platform for creating wondrous work.

I held the first Red Sneaker Writers conference in 2005. I invited the best speakers I knew, not only people who had published many books but people who could teach. Then I launched my small-group seminars—five intensive days working with a handful of aspiring writers. This gave me the opportunity to read, edit, and work one-on-one with people so I could target their needs and make sure they got what would help them most. This approach worked extremely well and I'm proud to say a substantial number of writers have graduated from my seminars and placed work with major publishers. But I realized not everyone could attend these seminars. How could I help those people?

This book, and the other books in this series, are designed to provide assistance to writers regardless of their location. The books are short, inexpensive, and targeted to specific areas where a writer might want help.

Let me see if I can anticipate your questions:

Why are these books so short? Because I've expunged the unnecessary and the unhelpful. I've pared it down to the essential information, useful ideas that can improve the quality of your writing. Too many instructional books are padded with excerpts and repetition to fill word counts required by book contracts. That's not the Red Sneaker way.

Why are you writing several different books instead of one big book? I encourage writers to commit to writing every day and to maintain a consistent writing schedule, and sometimes reading about writing can be an excuse for not writing. You can read the Red Sneaker books without losing much writing time. In fact, each can be read in a single afternoon. Take one day off from your writing. Read and make notes in the margins. See if that doesn't trigger ideas for improving your work.

I bet it will. And the next day, you can get back to your work.

You reference other books as examples, but you rarely quote excerpts from books (other than yours). Why?

Two reasons. First, I'm trying to keep these books brief. I will cite a book as an example, and if you want to look up a particular passage, it's easy enough to do. You don't need me to cut and paste it for you. Second, if I quote from materials currently under copyright protection, I have to pay a fee, which means I'd need to raise the price of the books. I don't want to do that. I think you can grasp my points without reading copyrighted excerpts. Too often, in my opinion, excessive excerpting in writing books is done to pad the page count.

Why does each chapter end with exercises?

The exercises are a completely integrated and essential part of this book, designed to simulate what happens in my small-group seminars. Samuel Johnson was correct when he wrote: *Scribendo disces scribere.* Meaning: You learn to write by writing. I can gab on and on, but these principles won't be concretized in your brain until you put them into practice.

So get the full benefit from this book. Take the time to complete the exercises. If you were in my seminar, this would be your homework. I won't be hovering over your shoulder when you read this book—but you should do the exercises anyway.

What else does the Red Sneaker Writers Center do?

I send out a free e-newsletter filled with writing advice, market analysis, and other items of interest. If you would like to be added to the mailing list, then please visit: http://www.williambernhardt.com/writing_instruction/index.php. I host an annual writing conference with a specific focus: providing the information you need to succeed. I lead small-group seminars in various cities each year. The newsletter will provide dates and information about these programs. And there will be future books in this series.

Okay, enough of the warm-up act. Read this book. Then write your story. Follow your dreams. Never give up.

William Bernhardt

CHAPTER 1: DEFINING PREMISE

The first thing you have to consider when writing a novel is your story, and then your story—and then your story!

Ford Maddox Ford

First let me explain what I mean by premise. Premise is the fundamental idea or core concept that underpins your story. It's that stray thought that wandered into your head one day while you were in the shower, or walking the dog (because the absence of outside noise allowed your subconscious to speak). Perhaps the idea seized you immediately, made you stop in your tracks and think, Wow, that would make a terrific novel. And you were likely right, because if the idea struck you as unique and worthy and exciting, it will likely strike someone else the same way. But don't stop with that initial idea. See if you can expand it and make it even better.

How do you improve that core concept? That's what this book is all about.

Premise is the fundamental idea or concept underpinning your story.

Today you often hear agents and editors say they are looking for a "high-concept" novel. What does that mean? Basically, it means they're looking for a book with a unique but compelling premise. Often, aspiring writers confuse "high-concept idea" with "good agent pitch," thinking they are one and the same. They are not. Writing conferences often recommend pitches that unite two successful (probably high-concept) works, leading to an endless stream of pitches involving the A + B = C formula. "It's *Star Wars* set in a *Blade Runner* universe," etc. John Grisham's breakthrough novel, *The Firm*, was originally sold as "*L.A. Law* meets *The Godfather.*" But the most engaging premises—and thus the most successful books—are not simply amalgams of previous hits. They're unique and interesting in their own right. So for now, instead of focusing on the pitch (which will be discussed in the last chapter), focus on how to write a good book with an engaging premise. You probably won't get that by reweaving the work of others. You need to devise an original premise that is so compelling readers feel that they have to read it.

Enriching the Core Idea

I'm often asked to provide the secret of getting published, and in my never-ending quest to be helpful, I usually provide an answer that is simpler and more honest than the asker wants. The secret of getting published is, first, to finish a book, second, to make it really good, and third, to never stop trying to get it to readers. Although this answer is completely accurate, it often frustrates the asker because they don't want to wait, or because they've been working hard and haven't had any success yet. I feel your pain. I was there for years, writing stuff I couldn't publish. Except in retrospect, I realize why my early work wasn't published. It wasn't very good. Not that the writing was poor (though it was far from flawless). I simply wasn't writing anything that would be of great interest to anyone other than myself. I hadn't hit upon that powerful premise, the sensational idea that would tickle readers' fancies just as much as it did mine.

Maybe you, like the students I see in my small-group seminars, have attended writing conferences and had the frustrating experience of pitching your work to editors and agents, which rarely turns out well for anyone. Here's what usually happens. You practice your pitch in the mirror for days, honing it to perfection, deliver it flawlessly, but still don't sell anything. Why? If the agent asks for your manuscript, but then several months later sends you an email saying, "Didn't grab me," it likely means they didn't think you wrote at a professional level yet, in which case I refer you to *Sizzling Style*. But far more frequently, aspiring writers don't even get that far. Their pitch is received with a complete lack of enthusiasm, even though you explained all its merits at great length. What was missing?

The premise didn't interest them.

This could mean they personally did not find the premise interesting enough, or that they thought it lacked commercial appeal. Either way, the result is the same. They don't ask to see your manuscript.

A strong premise is essential to selling stories to publishers—and readers.

How can you remedy this problem? By improving your premise.

Key Elements of Great Stories

In my book *Story Structure*, I asked the question: What are your three favorites stories of all time? Here I want to ask a variation on that question. Name three books you were desperately anxious to read. Skip the ones that

3

received excessive hype or were the third volume in a trilogy you'd already started. Identify the times you read the back cover copy and thought, I have got to read that book!

Okay, you've made your list. What do these books have in common?

You may see a continuing theme. You may see an appealing character type or setting. But there's a good chance you're seeing a strong premise. After all, if the premise didn't compel you to read it, why would you? Something made you pick up that book (unless it was required reading at school). How can you infuse your work-in-progress with a core idea as compelling as the one that caused you to read the three books you listed? Of course, it's much easier to talk about coming up with a breathtakingly original idea than to actually come up with one. But you're much more likely to come up with a promising idea if you understand what you're looking for. And that's the whole point of this book.

There are certain core elements you will find in all great stories. We could have a pleasant after-dinner chat debating what they are and how many there are, but I think almost anyone would agree there are at least three: Character, Setting, and Plot. All three are important, but the most important to the discussion of premise is usually Plot. When agents ask you to describe your high-concept story, they're asking for a plot description. When you pitch, you will probably focus primarily on plot. This does not mean that plot is more important than the character. It is not possible to have a successful story without interesting characters. I'm also not suggesting that premise is something separate and apart from character. But a careful consideration of premise will help you enrich your characters, will help you create characters that are more appealing to readers so you can make your book irresistible. **The distinctive elements that make great stories great involve character, setting, and plot.** I've written a previous book in this series discussing the importance of Character (*Creating Character*). The academic distinction between so-called character-driven books and plot-driven books is a canard. All great fiction is character-driven. Absent compelling characters, the plot is irrelevant. No one cares what happens to fictional stick figures. But a unique or compelling take on a character can only enhance your premise.

Here's another useful approach to enriching your premise: Identify the most successful, most enduring fictional characters of the last 150 years.

Let me be blunt. If this exercise is hard for you—you haven't read enough to be a writer. I'm not trying to be rude. I'm just stating a fact. It's not possible to be a great writer if you haven't read great writing. The writer must constantly fuel the engine, and that means reading, specifically reading quality work. Individual tastes may vary. But reading is essential.

Who are the best-known, most successful fictional characters? When I ask this question at writing seminars, the same names inevitably arise. Scarlett O'Hara. Or Harry Potter, if it's a younger crowd. Sherlock Holmes. James Bond. Tarzan. Superman.

What do these characters have in common?

They are all larger-than-life.

Larger-than-life characters engage the reader's imagination.

Scarlett isn't a fantasy character like Superman, but she's still not your run-of-the-mill Southern belle, nor does she much resemble most plantation gals of the era. Technically, she's not even a very nice person. Early on, she's self-centered and superficial. Even after times get hard, she's scheming, manipulative, and mean. Selfish. Greedy. Why are readers so devoted to her?

Because when the going gets tough, she gets tougher. She survives, unlike most of her neighbors. She doesn't get everything she wants, but she keeps that plantation intact. Just as we would like to think we might, given similar circumstances, though we also hope a situation never arises that tests this proposition.

Although arising from a dramatically different genre, Tarzan is a character similar to Scarlett in many ways. He, too, is thrust into difficult circumstances at a young age—as a baby, in fact. Orphaned in the wilds of Africa after his parents die, Tarzan is raised by the she-ape Kala. He's a hairless babe in a world of fierce baboons and most would not rate his chances at survival highly. But as it turns out, this lad has ingenuity and an inner strength that helps him endure. He discovers how to use a knife to compensate for his smaller teeth and less developed musculature. He teaches himself to read. His natural curiosity turns him into a survivor.

In the original author's hands, this may have been a story of "Blood will out." Tarzan was, after all, destined to be Lord Greystoke, a member of the British aristocracy. Put a lord in the jungle and guess what—pretty soon he's running the joint. But in today's more egalitarian era, I prefer to see this as a story of an exceptional character accomplishing exceptional deeds during difficult times.

Sherlock Holmes has an ability to use inductive reasoning to solve crimes. He sees what others miss. His extraordinary abilities turn out to be useful. Superman has powers beyond those of mortal men, which opens the doors to extraordinary adventures beyond those normally experienced by mortal men. Harry Potter has to go to school like all kids, but let's face it—his school is a lot cooler than the one we attended. And James Bond? Well, nobody does it better.

All of these characters have, to use the modern terminology, superpowers. Even Scarlett. They have gifts and qualities that allow them to do what we will probably never have an opportunity to do. They can say what we wish we'd said. Bond's morbid epigrams are perfect examples of repartee we only think of the next day. These characters express our deepest desires and fulfill our most exalted purposes.

They live our dreams.

Setting will be explored in greater detail in a future book, but for now, suffice to say that it is probably more important than you realize. Most beginning writers set their first novel where they live, in part because the central character is based upon themselves and the plot derives from their own experiences. And after all, if you set the book where you live, there will be less need for research. But you shouldn't be thinking about what setting will make your book easiest to write. You should be thinking about what setting will make your book irresistible to readers. What setting can become an important component of your powerful premise? There's no escaping the fact that some settings are more interesting than others. How can you know for sure? Trends and fashions come and go, but if a setting appeals to you, there's a good chance it will appeal to readers with similar tastes and interests.

Setting is a critical element of any great story.

In addition to being irresistible, your setting must also be convincing. The importance of credibility will be discussed later in this book, but for now, remember that it applies to setting as well as everything else. You must bring your fictional world to life in words. Please do not mistake this for suggesting that you can't create worlds that don't actually exist. Sometimes fantasy settings are the most intriguing of all. But if your setting does not exist (or if it is a historical era other than our own), then you must work especially hard to bring it to life. You must do your research. You must work through the ins and outs of your planet or fantasy universe till it seems coherent and logical. Your readers must believe in this world.

Part of the success of *The Hunger Games* series undoubtedly derives from the fact that this future dystopia, different from our world though it is, makes a certain sense. Blood sports, designed to keep the populace in line, go back at least as far as the Roman Empire. Stratification of society is nothing new. These familiar patterns, expanded and enriched with elements of fantasy, help make a fictional universe seem real. Ultimately, your readers must feel as if they have transported to another place. And that place must be a place they want to stay for a while, even if it is in many respects not an idyllic or even particularly pleasant place to be.

Sometimes perfectly ordinary places can become delightful through the skillful handling of a writer. One of my favorite writers, Mark Twain, did wonders with rural Missouri. Most people reading his books would normally have little desire to live in Hannibal, especially in that era, but Twain makes the poor, backward, bigoted, oppressive, slave-owning town seem like a lot of fun. Now that's good writing. Even today, thousands of people travel to Hannibal to walk the streets where it all supposedly took place.

Anyone who has read my Ben Kincaid novels may be sensing a certain inconsistency. You may be thinking, Hey, didn't you set those books in Tulsa, Oklahoma (a relatively short drive from Hannibal)? And weren't you living in Tulsa at the time? Wasn't this a classic example of a newbie writer setting his novels where he lives?

It certainly was. What can I say? I didn't know any better. And these excellent Red Sneaker books weren't around for me to consult. By the time I realized that a more exotic locale might've been a smarter move, it was too late. Ben's stomping ground had been established (although in some of the later books, I found excuses to send him to Chicago, Washington, D.C., etc.). To some degree, the geographical settings of these books may have been less important, because the real setting, the one that mattered, was the courtroom.

Many years ago, I had the opportunity to study at the University of Oklahoma with a writer named Jack Bickham. I was not the only one who did. His protégés included Jim Butcher, author of the famed Dresden Files novels. As the story goes, Butcher came up with this clever premise about an adult sorcerer having adventures, not in Middle Earth or some other fantasyland, but in contemporary USA. His original plan was to set the stories in Norman, Oklahoma, where he lived at the time. Bickham brought out a map of the nation and pointed. "There are three cities. New York, Chicago, Los Angeles. Pick one." As you may be aware, Butcher chose Chicago, though he had never visited the Windy City and made some (largely irrelevant) geographical errors in the early volumes. The series still took off.

Bickham's advice was the Old School wisdom of an earlier era. I've heard senior editors and agents say much the same thing at writer conferences. The idea is that people are more likely to buy books set where they live, so you want to choose a setting where a lot of people live. That may have worked at one time, but today, I think many readers are tired of books set in the Big Three, and possibly also San Francisco, Dallas, and Washington, D.C. Many readers are ready for something fresh, something that excites their imagination. That may not be your hometown, but it may be an intriguing locale that has an inherent connection to the story you want to tell.

The rest of this book will be a consideration of the elements you can inject into your premise to plus the plot. You need a fine setting with sympathetic characters, but what happens to those characters must be exciting and dramatic, out of the ordinary, and most importantly, meaningful. I've already written a book on Plot and I won't repeat it here, but if you're thinking that you're writing serious literary fiction so plot doesn't matter, you're wrong.

Timid storytelling rarely excites the imagination. A great story by definition involves great events. Stories are narratives, and while a literary novel may call for a different kind of plot, it still needs a plot, something that stirs the reader's imagination and resolves in a satisfying manner. This is why those books you put on your list earlier, why all great books, change lives. Because they combine setting, character, and plot to tell the reader something about humanity they might not have realized before.

Having established our foundation, we will now consider the key elements you can use to expand your core idea and make your book more appealing to editors, agents, and most importantly, readers. Those elements are:

POWERFUL PREMISE

1) Originality;
2) High Stakes;
3) Emotional Audience Appeal;
4) Readily Recognizable Conflict; and
5) Credibility.

Highlights

1) Premise is the fundamental idea or concept underpinning your story.

2) A strong premise is essential to selling stories to publishers—and readers.

3) The distinctive elements that make great stories involve character, setting, and plot.

4) Larger-than-life characters engage the reader's imagination.

5) Setting is a critical element of any great story.

Red Sneaker Exercises

1) You probably had some core idea for your story or novel before you began reading this book. What was it? Can you express it in a sentence or two?

2) Now that you have your premise down on paper, scrutinize it. Is it all that it could be? I'm going to ask you to continually reexamine it in light of the ideas discussed in the subsequent chapters. Does it seem too familiar? Is it too reminiscent of stories you've read before?

3) Have you chosen the setting that is best for the story, or the setting that is easiest for you to write? What would happen to this story if you set it somewhere else? Could the story take place in your favorite vacation spot?

Or someplace that's been in the news frequently? Or someplace you've always wanted to go but never been? What would happen to the story if you transplanted it somewhere else? Before you commit, make sure you've chosen the location that will allow you to tell this story to its best advantage.

4) Now let's think about the characters. The most important character is, of course, your protagonist. Even if you're writing a realistic story, have you created a protagonist who is in some respect larger than life? Even if you think the character's ordinariness is part of his or her appeal, is there some quality or talent that will allow the character to do what others do not, to succeed where others would fail? (And if there isn't, you may want to reconsider this character.) There must be some reason why this character completes the character arc or finishes the quest. What is it? Part of the appeal of fiction, and particularly genre fiction, is that it allows readers to be inspired by the deeds of heroic characters. What makes your protagonist unique?

5) Make sure you have a grasp of the fundamental idea behind your story before you proceed any further. Most of the subsequent discussion will be a consideration of how to improve it. So think about how the story will develop, working through the twists and turns, making it as interesting as you can, incorporating both the setting and characters to their maximum advantage. Do not be timid simply because you are new to writing. There may be a point where you've pushed your idea too far, but most early writers never get anywhere near it. Small events are not the stuff of great novels. As the kids say, Go big or go home.

Do not be afraid to enlarge your plot. Instead, ask yourself, How can I make this even bigger and better?

CHAPTER 2: SOMETHING OLD, SOMETHING NEW

Originality does not consist in saying what no one has ever said before, but in saying exactly what you think yourself.

James F. Stephan

I've often heard editors asked the standard question "What are you looking for?" or the more commercial variant "What are you buying?" Usually, the response is not helpful. Or in fact, it is helpful but the asker does not realize it, because it wasn't what they wanted to hear. More often than not, the answer is some variation of this: We're looking for the same, but different.

Decoded, this response means they're looking for work that fits into recognizable genres—How else would they market it?—but also has a new twist or variation on a theme, something that will attract interest and attention and could conceivably lead to word-of-mouth promotion, compulsive reading, and high sales.

Devising a genre plot is not that challenging. Turn on the television and you'll find about five hundred of them. But coming up with a fresh twist is something altogether more challenging. Those editors may say, "The same but different," as if the two were coequal, but we all know that the different is far more rare, far more difficult, and far more important.

Readers Yearn For Something They Have Not Seen Before

You've probably heard some cynical wag pontificating that there are no new plots (and by extension, no new settings, no new characters, etc.). In my book on Plot, I discussed what I called the five plots, but I was analyzing the progress of story in terms of the character's journey, not the events that take place along that journey. Rudyard Kipling once famously stated that there are only 69 plots, but he didn't explain what they were (I think he may have been kidding). Carlo Gozzi said there were 36 plots, one for each of the 36 distinct emotions. Ronald Tobias says there are twenty plots, no more, no less. If any of this is true, how do you come up with something readers haven't seen before?

Take a genre cliché and turn it upside-down.

Part of what you have to understand when you write fiction is that all genres have conventions that mirror their readers' expectations. Romance readers expect the couple to fall in love and hook up before the book ends. Crime readers expect the mystery to be solved and the criminal to be apprehended. Circumventing those genre expectations is usually not a good idea. Every few years someone puts out a book marketed as a "literary mystery" or "literary thriller," a combination of genres hoping to satisfy fans of both but more likely to satisfy fans of neither. "Look how sophisticated I am. I've written a mystery novel where the mystery isn't solved, just like in real life." And readers stay away in droves. People don't read novels because they're looking for more real life. They're looking for something better, something more satisfying.

It's still possible to do something interesting without undermining these fundamental expectations. What about another vampire novel, but this time, instead of it being a horror novel—it's a romance. And what if the vampires, instead of being old Hungarian dudes in dinner suits, are actually hunky teenage boys? And instead of burning up in the sunlight, they just sparkle? Yes, I'm describing the intensely successful *Twilight* novels, which capitalized upon the fondness of the young for supernatural stories, but made it original by transplanting it from one genre to another. The books were able to snare primarily female readers who still liked the supernatural but had outgrown Harry Potter and longed for something a little sexier. Stephanie Meyer did not invent the vampire novel, but she gave it an interesting spin. The same, but different.

Combine story elements in an unexpected way.

If you look at the books that have been huge breakout hits, you'll see many examples of books that took familiar tropes and injected some unusual or new element. (In the entertainment world, sometimes "new" is defined as "new for people whose memories only go back twenty years or so.") These books may involve unexpected combinations of story elements, for instance, a historical mystery. *The Alienist* scored big on the bestseller list a few years back. The plot was essentially another serial killer story, enhanced with a historical setting and the appearance of historical figures such as Teddy Roosevelt. George MacDonald Fraser's *Flashman* books are essentially a historical adventure series, but here the hero, rather than being the usual stalwart H. Rider Haggard manly man, is a scurrilous rake. And of course I have to mention a legal thriller series where the hero, rather than being the usual perfect brilliant

Perry Mason sort, is a bit of a nebbish (that's Ben Kincaid again).

You can see examples of the same principles in film. The comedy *Ruthless People* was basically an inversion of expectations that many thought original (though it was taken from an O. Henry story written eighty years before). The wife of a wealthy businessman is kidnapped and held for ransom. To everyone's surprise, the husband refuses to pay because he can't stand his wife and sees this as a chance to get rid of her without having to kill her himself. Now the kidnappers have a captive they don't want (and at one point, consider paying to get rid of).

In the Ron Howard film *Ransom*, the father of a kidnapped boy decides, instead of paying the ransom, to announce on national television that he's putting out a hit on the kidnappers. He'll pay anyone who ices them (an idea previously used in a earlier film of the same name and a television program). If you give this much thought, it makes little sense, as the kidnappers would likely just kill the boy and disappear. But the surprise had a powerful impact on viewers. The redneck appeal—"Yeah, stick it to those dirty criminals!"—struck a chord with many (especially if they didn't think too hard about it).

Going in Style was another bank heist picture, but with one important twist—this time, the robbers were senior citizens trying to prove they weren't washed up. The twist makes it more interesting as well as making the lead characters almost automatically sympathetic, despite being crooks.

The whole legal thriller phenomenon, so popular through the 1990s, was essentially the old school Erle Stanley Gardner mystery with more suspense elements in the mix. In other words, the courtroom drama was plussed

18

with the thriller. Instead of simply fighting for an innocent client, the lawyer often also fought for his own life.

The most popular mystery series of the last decade or so, *The Girl with the Dragon Tattoo* and its sequels, is another good example of "same but different." Plotwise, the first book is yet another serial killer story, worse, one preceded by about a hundred pages of financial intrigue that many found rather slow going. Question: What made these books so successful?

The Importance of Character

Answer: Lisbeth Salander. Because this character, who is not even the main character, was different. Mystery readers had not seen anything like her before, this young, underweight, tattooed, Goth girl with impaired social skills, sexual trauma, and an extremely troubled past. That was different. She also had extreme computer skills, but that was the least interesting part, because that skill, though necessary to the story, was one we'd seen before. I suspect I'm not the only reader who skimmed through the solo scenes with Mikael Blomkvist hoping for the reappearance of Lisbeth. She's the one who ultimately saves him, solves the case, and brings about her own form of rough justice. The American publisher, HarperCollins, immediately recognized what the strongest part of this series was. That's why they changed the original title (*Men Who Hate Women*) to a series of titles focusing on the most interesting part of the book: The Girl.

The key to breakout success is often a unique character.

As I write this, the most recent blockbuster series of books has been *Fifty Shades of Grey* and its sequels. The fantastic success of this series is usually attributed, especially by snob critics, to the S&M-flavored sex scenes. What these critics too often miss is that those sex scenes are "the different" but hardly the sole source of appeal. Porn has been with us since the ancient world (check out the graffiti in the ruins of Pompeii) and the Internet has made it easier to find than ever before. Most hardcore erotica doesn't sell that well. But at their core, the *Fifty Shades* books are romance novels, and romance novels have been popular throughout the twentieth century, at least since *Gone with the Wind*, and show no signs of slowing. In other words, yes, sex sells, but romance sells better.

Fundamentally, the three *Fifty Shades* novels tell a Cinderella story. There's a reason why, according to Bruno Bettelheim, Cinderella is the most popular fairy tale. The idea of the girl from nowhere with nothing being chosen for no apparent reason and turned into a princess has obvious appeal. Here, Anastasia (the very name suggests a princess) is a college literature student who loves to read but has little experience with men (you can already see the audience identification forming). For no apparent reason, the young yet incredibly rich and handsome Christian Grey takes a romantic interest in her and begins showering her with gifts, like a first-edition Thomas Hardy and a not-yet-released Mac computer (who wouldn't sleep with this guy?). Soon he's so into this girl that he's staying up all night just talking and braiding her hair. (So he has BFF cred in addition to being a sexual tiger.) Alas, as it turns out, his supreme self-confidence is but a façade. He's damaged goods, the product of a troubled past. Fortunately, Anastasia is a natural healer, so this becomes a mutually beneficial relationship and not just for the sex. He frees her

20

from her inhibitions and neuroses, and she heals his psychic damage.

Yes, there is an overarching message about allowing consenting adults to live outside the strictures of conformity and middle-class America. But even stronger, in my opinion, is the message about the redemptive power of love. By the end of the trilogy, Anastasia has married her prince, and although the author does not actually write the words "happily ever after," it is not hard to read them between the lines.

The most successful books tell stories with undercurrents that appeal to their readers.

I was not surprised to learn that *Fifty Shades of Grey* began its life as fan fiction involving *Twilight* characters. They both have similar appeals, and if you're going to learn lessons, you might as well learn from something that successfully captured the interest of millions of readers. Historically, romance novels have been popular with their core readers but have not marshaled much respect with the literary establishment. By cleverly integrating their romance stories with elements from other genres, in one case, horror, in the other, erotica, they were able to devise a unique work that still appealed to readers because the essential elements of the romance genre were present. Perhaps the authors planned this or perhaps they stumbled upon it by accident, but you don't want to rely on accidents. Instead, take your core idea and start thinking about how you can broaden its appeal, make your character more original, combine elements in a fresh manner, and turn an ordinary premise into an irresistible one.

I would never advise any writer to do anything they dislike or find distasteful just to make their work more commercial. But if you can come up with an idea that does

21

intrigue you and also broadens the appeal of the book, that's a win-win.

Great writers always stand on the shoulders of those who came before them. This is your chance to put your lifetime of reading to good use. Take a good idea, give it an ingenious twist, and make it even better.

POWERFUL PREMISE

Highlights

1) Readers yearn for something they have not seen before.

2) Take a genre cliché and turn it upside-down.

3) Combine story elements in an unexpected way.

4) The key to breakout success is often a unique character.

5) The most successful books tell stories with undercurrents that appeal to their readers.

Red Sneaker Exercises

1) This is the point where you have to think about, not simply what story do I want to write, but what story do I think might appeal to readers (and thus editors and agents). Can you tweak your main character, or a secondary character, to give them, say, more Lisbeth and less you? Who's the most interesting person you know? When was the last time you were stopped cold by someone doing something unexpected? Is it possible to get some of that into one of your characters?

2) What are the genres you read most frequently? Can you combine them in a new and interesting way? If one of your choices was "literary fiction," then beware. Most attempts to crossbreed literary with genre fiction fail,

because the uniqueness of literary fiction has so much to do with the use of language and so little to do with the plot (though there must be one). But attempts to cross-pollinate elements from different traditional storytelling fields often result in new and interesting results. Can you put many of the things you most enjoy reading about into one story?

3) Every story has a message, an overarching theme or idea. Maybe this is the life lesson the protagonist learns as a result of the book's journey. Maybe this is a virtue or trait or priority that results in triumph. In any case, books with positive and appealing underlying messages are far more likely to appeal to readers. What's the message of your story? Can you write it out in a sentence or two?

CHAPTER 3: RAISING THE STAKES

Finishing a book is just like you took a child out in the backyard and shot it.

Truman Capote

I f I were to suggest one change that more than anything else is likely to improve the appeal of your work-in-progress, it would be this: Raise the stakes. Too often beginning writers think timidly. This is somewhat understandable. When you have never written much less published anything, it seems somewhat presumptuous to concoct an epic multi-part generational saga set in a quasi-historical fantasy world of your own creation. And yet, a small story involving characters based upon you and your friends (and your enemies, appearing as evildoers) is unlikely to lead to great success. If your reader feels there is not much going on, or not much of consequence, they are unlikely to feel compelled to read the book. Granted, not every book needs to involve the coming apocalypse or the threat of World War III. But whatever the story you've chosen to tell, it will be more compelling if your readers feel that it matters, that the outcome matters, that something important is at stake.

High stakes yield high success.

Size Matters

In the typical romance, the ultimate question is whether the male and female leads will fall in love, consummate, and marry. But is that all there is to it? In the typical mystery story, the ultimate question is who did it, and why, and will the killer be caught? But is that enough to hold a reader's interest? In a thriller, the ultimate question may be whether the innocent man on the lam, or the heroic rogue agent with secret information, will prevail. But if there is nothing on the table except whether these obvious questions will be answered, you may find it difficult to attract an audience. Because at the end of the day, if the reader chooses to think consciously about it, they know that romantic couple will fall in love, the mystery will be solved, and the thriller series character will not die.

So why bother reading the book?

There must be something more. And the *more* more, the better.

What's at risk in your story? What happens if the protagonist doesn't succeed? Is there more than just the mystery isn't solved or the couple doesn't snuggle? There should be. No matter how big your stakes are at present, they can always be bigger. How you should enlarge them, of course, depends upon the type of story you're writing. Not every book needs to open with a bomb exploding or to end with the world on the brink of nuclear annihilation. On the other hand, if you're writing that kind of international thriller, that might work. You have to do what's right for your story. The stakes may be external and public. They may be internal and private. Whatever they are, make them as big as they can possibly be.

You probably already know that there are many levels of conflict. I have divided conflict into three categories: external, internal, and personal. External deals with public

26

stakes—what impact will this story have on the world. Internal and personal conflicts concern the stakes to the characters, primarily the protagonist. And in all cases, the bigger the stakes, the more dramatic the conflict, the more engaging the book.

To increase the public stakes, ask yourself: How could things get worse than they already are?

To increase the private stakes, ask yourself: How could this matter more than it already does?

And to have the best book possible, increase both.

An important fundamental of plotting is understanding that the suspense should increase as the book progresses. Your protagonist should be subjected to increasingly dire predicaments with each chapter. The thumbscrews should tighten. And that means more events must occur to intensify those conflicts. You want to lock your character into the struggle, or quest, or dilemma, with such high stakes that they cannot abandon the fight (though they have increasingly smaller chances of success). That kind of plotting makes for a riveting book. When readers can see that built into the premise, when it drips from the description on the back of the book or the paragraph under the cover on the Amazon page, there's an excellent chance that book will be bought.

Another problem aspiring writers often face when pitching their books to editors and agents is the blank stare reaction. I have seen Donald Maass respond to pitches with "So?" or "So what?" or "Why should I care?" Too often the pitcher has no response because they haven't really thought about it in advance.

Do you have an answer? You should. If you've made the stakes big enough, these should be easy questions to answer. If they aren't, you've got some work to do.

27

Increasing the private stakes means making the reader care more about the character by showing what the character cares about. This is important on many levels, because after all, if the reader doesn't care about the protagonist, none of the plotting matters. They can run and jump and shoot all they want. Readers won't care. But show that the character is fighting for a greater cause, risking his life to save a kidnapped daughter, trying to reconcile with a parent before it's too late, reaching out to an estranged wife, and suddenly the reader cares.

Ask yourself: If the protagonist does not succeed, what would be lost? Could he lose more? Up the ante. And make sure the stakes will be important to the reader.

Stakes don't matter unless they are connected to underlying human values.

There are many ways of creating human worth, of giving readers a sense that this fight is worth fighting. Freedom, honesty, integrity, loyalty, bravery, love—just to name a few. These are time-honored and universally cherished values that have fueled many a successful story.

Can you incorporate those values into a character or plot development that will give your story a larger perspective? What if instead of merely solving a mystery or pursuing the selfish desire for a romantic partner, the quest takes on a larger meaning, because it means more to the protagonist, his family, or the world. That will make your story stand out. That will make the book seem more important, more worth reading, because you've raised the stakes in an emotionally powerful manner.

Stakes That Matter

Let's face it, some struggles are just more important than others. Once upon a time, all you had to do to motivate a thriller was suggest that the Russians might get some secret microfiche. For an audience mired in the Cold War, that had lived through the Rosenberg trials and seen the fear created by stolen secrets, that was enough. After the Berlin Wall fell, it stopped being enough. Thrillers faded until Dan Brown created something new, a thriller that gravitated around historical and religious truths—high stakes because of the impact they could have on a world of believers. Today, thrillers increasingly involve plots that would have gotten them shelved in the science fiction section twenty years ago. Too often these books posit end-of-the-world-as-we-know-it scenarios, which occasionally work, but too often don't.

This is what I call the *Star Trek: Generations* mistake (thus providing my mandatory *Star Trek* reference). In that movie, Malcolm McDowell (who also played Flashman in an earlier movie) threatens to destroy an entire solar system unless Kirk and Picard stop him. Billions of lives will be lost. The problem is—we don't know any of those people. Not even Kirk and Picard know those people. It's just numbers. It's not tied to basic human values, except the broad principle that life is sacred, perhaps. As Stalin once grimly remarked, "A single death is a tragedy. A million deaths is a statistic." That movie would've been more dramatically compelling if Malcolm had threatened one person the captains knew and loved, say, a romantic interest or offspring.

The most dramatic stakes are personal stakes— stakes that affect people we care about.

John D. McDonald once famously defined story as "Stuff happens to people you care about." This is a good definition (and one worth remembering when you're preparing that agent pitch). Obviously, if the reader doesn't care, the story is sunk. But when the protagonist has more reason to care, you have higher stakes, and thus, a more engaging story. Compare these premises:

A firefighter races to save a burning building from destruction.

A firefighter races to save 68 people trapped on the top floor of a burning building.

A firefighter, dismissed for bucking regulations to help a teenage girl, races to save 68 people trapped on the top floor of a burning building.

And finally…

A firefighter, dismissed for bucking regulations to save a teenage girl from a life in prison, races against the clock to save 102 people trapped on the top floor of a burning building—including his pregnant wife.

Gets better each time, huh? And not just because there are more words. Those words were added for a reason. Each new phrase intensified the stakes. Each addition either made the situation direr or gave the protagonist more reason to fight. And as a result, each addition gave the reader more reason to care about the story.

Okay, the whole firefighter premise is a little trite, but you didn't think I was going to use a good idea on an example, did you?

POWERFUL PREMISE

The Importance of Pacing

Another good reason to improve your premise is that it will inevitably make it easier for you to write the book when the time comes. The more you have to write about, the quicker the chapters will come. Pacing is critical to all fiction. I've heard Steve Berry say, Story never takes a vacation, and he's right. You cannot let the tension slack, not for a second, if you want to hang on to your readers. That will be much easier to achieve if you've front-loaded your premise with many different stakes-raising elements. Then you'll have no trouble filling those chapters with foreshadowing, foreboding, and suspense.

Another friend of mine defines writing as: Torturing your characters for fun and profit. There's much truth in that. It's a devious sort of entertainment. As you're devising these stakes-raising events, find ways of showing your readers why the protagonist is in fact the protagonist of this book, rather than some other person. In a previous chapter, we discussed the possibility of giving your protagonists unique abilities. Make sure you've created stakes-raising dilemmas that will give them opportunities to use those abilities. Let that explain why this character succeeded where others failed. High stakes give your characters a chance to rise to the occasion, to surmount incredible odds.

The tagline for *Jaws IV: The Revenge* has become notorious as a result of all the subsequent parodies: This time its personal. The idea of a shark attacking out of vengeance struck many as silly. And yet, I can see what the filmmakers were going for. The flaw with having a shark as your protagonist is that it's a one-dimensional character and at some point not much of an opponent for forewarned smarties. Make it a personal grudge match, and the drama intensifies.

This "personal" approach to heightening the drama, especially in the final act, has become somewhat cliché in Hollywood. The problem, often, is that the personal stakes don't seem connected to the main story but more like something clumsily injected at the last minute. In most of the *Die Hard* movies, for instance, the stakes become personal toward the end even though they never were before. The story starts out pitting John McClane against some evil baddie, but toward the end something occurs to threaten the life of his wife (#2) or his daughter (#4) or his son (#5). Prior to that, we barely even knew these characters existed.

The best way to increase personal stakes is to give the protagonist more to lose. Make it personal by introducing those characters early and making the bond between them real and important throughout the story, even before their lives are on the line. The more personal the stakes, the more likely they are to resonate with readers. Since story is when stuff happens to people we care about—give us more reason to care.

POWERFUL PREMISE

Highlights

1) High stakes yield high success.

2) To increase the public stakes, ask yourself: How could things get worse than they already are?

3) To increase the private stakes, ask yourself: How could this matter more than it already does?

4) Stakes don't matter unless they are connected to underlying human values.

5) The most dramatic stakes are personal stakes—stakes that affect people we care about.

Red Sneaker Exercises

1) Can you make the stakes in your work even greater by adding a personal component? In other words, this time make it personal. The more personal, the better.

2) Think through your plan for your book, how you see the story unfolding. Can you pinpoint the places where the stakes escalate as the story progresses? The stakes should first become apparent when the inciting incident occurs (see *Story Structure* if this term is unfamiliar to you). But that's just the start. The stakes should escalate throughout the book. Resist the temptation to throw out everything at once. Let the stakes accrete chapter by chapter. Let the problems become incrementally worse. Save something truly awful for the end of Act Two. Don't

stop until you've defined at least five different places where the stakes increase significantly.

3) Imagine that you've just delivered your pitch to Donald Maass and that famous agent stares back at you and says, "Why should I care?"
What's your answer?

CHAPTER 4: EMOTIONAL APPEAL

There are some subjects that can only be tackled in fiction.

John Le Carre

Great books often leave readers with a wide range of emotional responses. Think about your all-time favorite books. What was your emotional response when you read them? Did you laugh? Did you cry? Did you feel inspired? Those responses do not occur by accident (at least not usually). They occur because the writer created a premise that touched on fundamental human emotions and virtues, like sacrifice, and honor, and love.

You want a premise that gets people where they live. You want a premise that sucker-punches them in the gut.

Today, in some circles, it's considered less sophisticated or literary to write something that produces an emotional response. Such stories are sometimes described as "sentimental" or "manipulative," and it isn't a compliment. As great a writer as he was, John Steinbeck sometimes had to defend his literary reputation against the charge of sentimentality.

When did touching human emotions become a bad thing? Sentimentality only fails when it is artificially imposed on a work that hasn't earned it. I hope I never become so sophisticated or literary that I prefer strictly intellectual experiences over emotional ones. Even Faulkner described the key to good writing as "the human heart in conflict with itself." How on earth did we become so snooty or so concerned about being considered literary that emotion became a negative element? Producing emotional responses is one reason great stories have a transformative or cathartic effect on their readers. Who doesn't recall crying at the end of *Jane Eyre* ("Reader, I married him.")? Or *Tess of the D'Urbervilles?* Or *The Notebook?* Or laughing over *Tom Jones* or *The Devil Wore Prada?* Or for that matter, *Green Eggs and Ham?* Who didn't feel inspired and supercharged at the end of *Gone With the Wind?* If you can shape a premise designed to stir these kinds of emotions, your book is far more likely to be a success.

Great stories stir the emotions and touch the heart.

The Human Heart

Trying to decode the human heart is a complicated matter and far beyond my feeble powers. But I believe we can safely say that one reason people read stories, and novels in particular, is for the cathartic experience. You may have heard readers try to justify their reading habits by using the word "entertainment" or "escapism." Sadly, I hear this most often when readers feel insecure. When the avid romance reader is caught thumbing through them at the grocery, too often she says, "Well, sometimes I just like to read something quick and easy." When not rereading James Joyce, presumably. Too often at book signings people have handed me one of my mysteries or legal dramas saying, "My mother just loves those things." Of course. Who would've ever thought you would sink so low as to buy those things for yourself?

But if you're looking at the statistics, you know that people are in fact buying those things for themselves. Except for children's literature, most books are bought by the person who intends to read them. The *Twilight* phenomenon was initially written off as pulp fiction for teenagers read by teenagers. Then someone did a study and found that more than half of those mothers "buying the book for their daughters" were actually reading the books themselves. Apparently this supernatural romantic fantasy had some appeal to grown-up readers as well. The appeal of exotic, dangerous, but fulfilling love is virtually universal. Why wouldn't adults want to read about it? Should we really be surprised that romance novels continue to dominate adult genre fiction?

Don't make the mistake of thinking the appeal of romance is solely for women, either. Give it somewhat less embarrassing packaging, something without the bare-chested Adonises and apparently nursing mothers and it turns out men are not immune to the appeal of romance. Why else would *The Bridges of Madison County* become such a stratospheric success in the 90s? It was well-packaged and affordably priced, but most importantly, the covers were such that a male could hold it in his hands without complete embarrassment. This was not the first time this phenomenon had ever occurred. About twenty years before, *Love Story* by Erich Segal, another slight but romantically tragic tale, soared to the top of the bestseller lists, crossing boundaries to great success. These books were bought by both genders, and that's the secret to their breakthrough success. Turns out, touching human emotions is a good way to sell books.

Today, Nicholas Sparks is writing romantic heartbreak on a regular basis, both in books and for Hollywood, and finding great success. Ironically, even when readers/viewers go in knowing full well there will be tragedy, they still turn out for the experience. They probably wouldn't volunteer for pain and suffering in their real lives. But experiencing these powerful emotions through a fictional character is a different matter altogether. That cathartic purging can be healthy and cleansing. More than anything else, I believe, today many people just want to feel *something*.

Our post-industrial, post-computer, modern society has distanced people from the emotions that used to be central to everyday life. You hear about people needing to "get in touch with their emotions" or to "get out of their heads" or to "be in the moment." A good book puts the reader in an emotionally charged situation and allows them to experience those emotions through the safety filter of a fictional character. As real as that character may seem, it only exists on the printed page, and you can close that book at any time. But that's not what we do. Give us a good story and we stay up reading all night and feel regret when the story is over. People seek out those powerful emotional experiences. So give them what they want.

Readers seek a cathartic experience, that is, they want to experience powerful emotions through a fictional character.

A Moment of Inspiration

I'm always pleased when one of my writing exercises leads to someone telling me how literature has influenced their life. Most impressive is when they tell me how a book changed the way they thought, the way they viewed the world. In other words, a story, fictional though it may be, influenced real life. That has happened time and again throughout our recorded history. The works of Charles Dickens repeatedly led to tangible social reform. Books like *Oliver Twist* and *Nicholas Nickleby* led to better laws governing public schools and workhouses. In the US, Upton Sinclair's *The Jungle* led to dramatic reform of the meat-packing industry.

Great stories stir great responses.

Of course, the most profound example of this is *Uncle Tom's Cabin*. Sometimes modern students mistakenly get the impression this book must be nonfiction, but it wasn't. It was a novel—a thriller, in fact. Was any scene more suspenseful Eliza's daring escape? Was anything more heart-wrenching than Simon Legree whipping poor Tom? Many contemporary critics had little respect for it. But it had a profound impact on its readers. For many, having an author put them inside the head of a slave was an eye-opening experience. They could cathartically experience the pain and desperation of a slave, as well as their strength and abiding faith. It was an emotional experience, and not at all a pleasant one, but it left a powerful footprint. As a result, this novel accomplished what decades of sermons and politics could not.

Readers love vicarious life lessons.

You have probably heard the term "takeaway." In the world of fiction, this is not a reference to what you're picking up for dinner. It's a reference to what, if anything, your readers will take home after the book is finished. Yes, you want to give them spellbinding suspense or heartwarming romance. But is there more? Is there something that makes them laugh or cry, that makes their heart swell? I hope there is, because that's the hallmark of the most successful books.

Any book tapping into the primal emotions is likely to succeed. A good cry is a cleansing experience. A good laugh is also restorative. Acts of heroism can elevate the spirit. And it is possible to combine these and have elements of both or many. Carl Hiassen's extremely popular novels are typically described as mysteries, but without question there are more laughs than you'll find in Lee Child or Phillip Margolin. Some readers are able to experience both responses, sometimes simultaneously. One can be a release for the other. At the movies, an action-packed chase or fight scene will often be followed by some witty riposte. "Shocking," Bond says, just after he electrocutes his assailant, and the laughter releases the tension (and prevents you from thinking about nagging details like what he's going to do about the corpse in his bathtub).

Perhaps the most powerful takeaway is to instill in readers a feeling of inspiration. This might take the form of changing a reader's views on social or political issues. It might be a more spiritual experience. We all would like to feel heroic—why else have we thrilled to the exploits of heroic figures, literally since the dawn of stories. Reading about fictional characters like Odysseus and Gilgamesh and Beowulf makes us want to be better than we are, to be more heroic, to act less selfishly.

You will probably not be surprised to hear that reading can have a positive effect on readers. A recent study indicated that, contrary to the stereotype of readers as shy, reserved folk out of touch with reality, reading left people more compassionate and with a better understanding of others. As a result of vicariously experiencing fictional viewpoints, readers were more likely to show and better equipped to express empathy. Reading, in short, left them better able to love.

Great stories will inspire their readers.

Let me give you two classic examples. You've probably read what is perhaps Dickens's most popular novel *A Tale of Two Cities* (and if you haven't, now's the time). "It was the best of times, it was the worst of times." Or to be more precise, tolerable in London, disastrous in Paris. The novel centers around Sydney Carton, a likeable but dissipated, alcoholic lawyer in London. He adores the young and beautiful Lucy, who is kind to him, but at the end of the day, he's just not husband material. She marries another man who, interestingly enough, looks very like Carton. Let me cut to the chase: Lucy's husband is captured by French revolutionaries during the Reign of Terror and is thrown into the Bastille, soon to be executed. This changes everything for Carton. A lesser man might think, Hey, here's my chance with Lucy, the husband is about lose his head. But not our hero. He instead takes advantage of the great similarity in their appearance, sneaks into the Bastille, and takes his lookalike's place. The husband returns to England and Carton goes to the guillotine, not filled with self-pity or remorse, but instead thinking, "It is a far, far better thing that I do, than I have ever done. It is a far, far better rest that I go to, than I have ever known."

What reader wouldn't be inspired by that? And this is not errant heroism just for the sake of being heroic or simply bringing down a bad guy. This is a man showing what it means to truly love another person. This is, ultimately, a romantic novel, but one that strikes a more powerful and universal note than most, because the ending seems to have led to something greater and more important than simply two people who like each other living happily ever after. This is not a happy ending as such, and yet, one finishes it feeling energized and enriched by the experience. The reader closes the book and feels that, instead of simply passing the time, the book has made them a better person, a person with a clearer sense of right and wrong and how a person should spend their time on this planet.

My other favorite example is *Les Miserables*, one of the greatest novels of all time. You may think you know the story based upon exposure to the musical or a film, but let me tell you, if you haven't read the novel, you've cheated yourself (though I think it is perhaps permissible to skip Hugo's digressions into history and politics and just read the story).

This massive work has many subplots, but the main story revolves around Jean Valjean, a man imprisoned for stealing bread to help his sister's starving children. He serves nineteen years hard labor for that crime and his frequent unsuccessful escape attempts. When finally released, he is given parole documents to carry at all times, making it virtually impossible to get work. The only person who shows him any kindness is an elderly bishop, and he rewards this man by stealing his plates and flatware. When the gendarmes drag Valjean back to the bishop (Valjean must be the worst thief/escape artist of all time), rather than pressing charges, the bishop says, basically, "Dude, you forgot the candlesticks. I wanted you to have those, too." The gendarmes leave. And the bishop tells Valjean, "Now your life belongs to God."

Valjean tears up his parole papers so he can start a new life and he devotes it to helping his fellow humans. He adopts Cosette, the orphaned daughter of the tragic Fantine, and despite the constant persecution of Javert, hounding him because he broke parole, he manages to raise her and make sure she has a better life than he did. He risks his own life at the barricade to rescue Cosette's fiancé. His life acquires meaning through his love of his adopted daughter. He has fulfilled the bishop's directive by doing what God would have him do—live a life dedicated to others. "To love another person is to see the face of God."

Yes, there has been heroism, and romantic adventure of the old-fashioned variety. But most importantly, there has been inspiration. As in *Tale of Two Cities*, ultimately, this story is about what it means to love.

Great stories show us how to live and how to love.

Probably few readers got to the end of either of these books without shedding a tear or two. And probably few closed the book without feeling a rush of joy swelling within them. How can you read about these heroic achievements without wanting to do the same? A great takeaway causes readers to recommend the book to their friends. And that's what you want.

An essential part of your pre-planning should focus on the premise, and an important part of sharpening your premise should concern the takeaway. Yes, it's possible something might occur to you while you write the story, but the best writers will not leave something so important to chance. Better to go into the novel with a sound idea about the takeaway, and then see how the writing of the book provides clarity and additional opportunities to bring it to life. When you write a book that touches fundamental human emotions, you not only increase your chances of success, but also invite the possibility of penning one of those magic treasured books that stick with readers long after the reading experience has ended. Charles Dickens remain fantastically popular a century and a half after his death. Victor Hugo's funeral was attended by millions. And the takeaway of their work still resonates today.

POWERFUL PREMISE

Highlights

1) Great stories stir the emotions and touch the heart.

2) Readers seek a cathartic experience, that is, they want to experience powerful emotions through a fictional character.

3) Great stories stir great responses.

4) Readers love vicarious life lessons.

5) Great stories will inspire their readers.

6) Great stories show us how to live and how to love.

Red Sneaker Exercises

1) Reflect upon your most satisfying and influential reading experiences. Do they have a common takeaway? It's possible they all led to purely intellectual experiences, but more likely that they led to emotional ones. Did they allow you to expunge emotions, or become inspired, or feel love coursing through your veins?

Now ask yourself what elements you might add to the premise for your work to produce that same takeaway. Do you need to add a love interest? A family? Can you create a scene that makes it clear that your protagonists serve a person or cause greater than themselves?

2) Although publishers will always encourage their writers to provide the traditional happy ending, often the most memorable stories do not wrap up so tidily. Rick does not get Ilsa, Scarlett does not get Rhett, Darnay does not get Lucy—and yet, these stories end on an upbeat rather than tragic note, because something inspirational has taken the place of disappointment, such as Rick's commitment to fighting the Nazis, Scarlett's determination to save Tara, Darnay's self-sacrifice. Can you instill something that powerful into your premise?

CHAPTER 5: READILY RECOGNIZABLE CONFLICT

People aren't born good or bad. Maybe they're born with tendencies either way, but it's the way you live your life that matters.

Cassandra Clare

As you are likely well aware, stories center around conflict. Without conflict, there is no story. And by conflict, I don't necessarily mean people are shouting at each other all the time. I mean there is something the protagonist wants but is not getting (at least immediately). There is an unsatisfied goal or desire. And more often than not, conflict is attributable to the opposing goals of differing people or entities. The more readily recognizable that conflict is, the more immediately apparent it is, the sharper your premise will be. When people can hear you describe the premise in a sentence or two and immediately think, *Wow, I can see where that's going*, or *I can see why that's a big problem*—then you know you have a winning premise.

Inherent Conflict

Some conflicts have to be explained, and in the most difficult books, they have to be explained at length. If you're having trouble making people understand why your antagonist poses a threat, there's something wrong with your premise and it needs to be refined. If everyone gets it right off the bat, then you know you have a winner.

Readily recognizable conflict leads to an exciting premise.

You have perhaps seen or heard about the television game show called *The Amazing Race*. As so-called reality programs go, it's less offensive than some. Basically, pairs of contestants race across the globe and the first team to reach the finish line wins the big prize.

In most races, people race alone. But on this television show, people race in pairs. Why?

Conflict, that's why. This program isn't scripted (exactly) so how do they keep viewers watching? By editing to emphasize the conflict. One person racing alone, you might have to guess what's going on inside their head. But two people racing together will talk, and if they have to reach consensus on important decisions with high stakes and a ticking clock—that's inevitably going to create conflict. Those moments when people blow up and yell at each other are what these shows are all about.

But getting to the point of this chapter—have you also noticed that these twosomes are not chosen at random?

Occasionally you get two longtime pals or siblings or other such natural pairings. But more often you get...the Baptist preacher and his lesbian daughter. Or the divorced couple thinking about reuniting for the sake of the kids. Or co-workers who both wanted the same position but one got it and the other was bitter about it. Why?

Because these pairings have inherent conflict. The conflict is built into the description. No one has to go on at length about why these duos might produce sparks. As soon as you hear (at the top of each episode) that the team is a preacher and his lesbian daughter, you've already assimilated the potential for conflict.

It's built into the premise. And that increases the average viewer's interest in the program.

It should be built into your premise as well. You do not create characters randomly. You create characters to maximize the conflict. To give yourself more to write about. To give the characters more to worry about. And to give the readers more reasons to read.

Conflict should be built into the premise.

Think how much simpler your agent pitch will be if you don't have to spend much time explaining the conflict. As soon as you describe the protagonist and antagonist, or the protagonist and his sidekick, the agent's eyes light, a grin spreads over her face, and she says, Oh my. I can see the problem.

That's the kind of premise that gets people reading and buying books.

Agenda Conflict

Once upon a time, most thrillers and adventure stories had a fundamental premise: there is a good guy and a bad guy, and we're rooting for the good guy. Today, this seems a little too comic book for serious fiction or, for that matter, even for comic books. Just describing someone as "bad" seems too simplistic.

In the real world, no one thinks they're the bad guy. To the contrary, everyone believes they're the hero of their own story. Even the people who committed some of the vilest acts in history did not think they were villains. In America, at one time, it was common to denigrate those who dropped the bombs on Pearl Harbor. After all, they perpetrated a sneak attack that took many lives. Did those pilots think they were bad guys? Far from it. They thought they were national heroes. You can't get people to fly kamikaze planes unless you convince them they're fighting for a noble cause. In their minds, America was the oppressor, trying to control Japan, so the bombing was a blow for national freedom.

If you've visited Pearl Harbor over the past decades, you may have noticed how the treatment of this historic event has changed. At one time, the exhibits had a strong anti-Japanese flavor. Today, the surround-sound film everyone sees before they travel to the Arizona Memorial treats the Japanese cause with considerably greater sympathy, discussing the effect of the embargoes and the plan to spread the Japanese empire across the Pacific. This change reflects the modern attempt to try to understand history rather than reducing it to good guys and bad guys. Ideally, your fiction will reach for the same level of sophistication.

Even the people who flew planes into the World Trade Center did not consider themselves to be bad guys. This is probably the most horrific incident to occur on American soil in the history of this nation, and certainly in the aftermath you could hear all kinds of negative comments about anyone of Middle Eastern persuasion. But did those hijackers consider themselves evil? No. They considered themselves political and religious heroes. They were convinced they fought for a greater cause and any loss of life was justified, perhaps even Allah-approved. They apparently believed they were going to heaven where they would be treated to a large number of virgins. (Though I note the Koran does specify the gender of those virgins. Those guys could be in for a big surprise.)

Agenda conflict makes a stronger premise than evil.

Since in real life, no one thinks they're the bad guy, perhaps in your fiction, it's too simplistic to create antagonists who are just evil. Or greedy. Or crazy. Or on drugs. Or any other shorthand designation that prevents you from creating characters with actual depth or realistic motivation.

Instead of relying on bad guys, try creating agenda conflict. Agenda conflict is a term borrowed from the world of psychology. Agenda conflict recognizes that people can have opposing views without one of them being evil. They simply want different things. And that creates inherent, inescapable conflict. They may well both be right, at least from their own perspective. The best conflicts allow readers to see that each of the competing forces has a valid point of view. We will always root for the protagonist. That's built into the nature of storytelling. But when readers can see where the antagonist is coming from, you'll have a stronger story. What's more, because the conflict is so inherent, so deeply etched, the reader knows it will be difficult, challenging, if not impossible to resolve. And that will lead to a more dramatic and engaging story.

The strongest premise involves strong opposing forces that have understandable but conflicting desires.

A World in Conflict

Fortunately, this kind of inherent conflict is not that difficult to find. For good or ill, we live in a world replete with conflict. Why do so many works of fiction, particularly literary fiction, revolve around family conflicts? Because they are so prevalent in real life, infinite in variation but always worth reading about. Virtually the entire oeuvre of the wonderful Pulitzer-Prize winning author Anne Tyler revolves around family conflicts. Parent-child relationships. Sibling rivalries. Husband-wife controversies. They appear so often in fiction because they occur so often in life.

For that matter, rarely has anyone told a military story that didn't involve some strife between divisions, or branches, or between superior officers (who are usually wrong) and lesser officers (who are usually right—in fiction). Thus we have inherent conflict. Political stories, like my novel *Capitol Threat*, typically involve conflicts between branches of the government. Executive branch vs legislative. Legislative vs. judicial. These stories involve inherent conflict because, after all, why do these different branches exist except to interfere with one another? The principle of checks and balances revolves around the need for one division of the government to restrain another.

Politicians and scientists clash over the cause of climate change or Oklahoma earthquakes. Teachers and preachers clash over what should be taught in science class. A class-stratified society argues about whether special treatment should be granted to the haves or the have-nots. This world is rife with inherent conflict. If you can inject that into your story, in an interesting or unique manner, you'll have a stronger premise.

In my novel, *Dark Eye*, the main protagonist is Susan Pulaski, who's trying to catch a killer known as "Edgar," because his deeds are inspired by the works of Edgar Allan Poe. Edgar is not killing people in bizarre recreations of scenes from Poe's stories just because he's evil, or just because he's crazy. (A common modern substitute that similarly substitutes for valid, compelling motivation.) I won't go into why Edgar has become the person he is (though the book does). But my point is that he has what to him is a strong motivation for his crimes. Though his close readings of Poe's cosmological work *Eureka*, he has become convinced that his crimes will take us all to Dreamland, a paradisiacal world Poe wrote about. To Edgar, Poe is the L. Ron Hubbard who showed the path to a better world. Like all such exoduses, the path will not be easy, but he's willing to undertake the sacrifice to get us all to the promised land. In other words, Edgar thinks he's the good guy. He's the hero, the Christ-figure making incredible sacrifices for his fellow man, and as a result, he fights all the harder to prevent Susan from interfering with his work. To me, this makes for a much more interesting premise than the standard "good guy vs. bad guy" or "sane hero vs. crazy person."

Clint Eastwood's best film, *Unforgiven*, has a similar motif. In this western, which seems to sendup the traditional Man With No Name western that made Eastwood a superstar, the divisions between good guys and bad guys are particularly murky. We automatically empathize with Eastwood's character because he's our protagonist (and we've seen him at home raising his kids and some pigs) but his actions become increasingly less "good guy" as the story develops. On the other hand, the erstwhile antagonist, a local sheriff played by Gene Hackman, is not a bad person. He's friendly, conscientious, and tries to do the right thing. He's building a house near the lake. He perhaps errs when he insufficiently punishes two men who lacerate prostitutes, but at least he's trying. When Eastwood comes to town determined to execute those men, there is agenda conflict. They each want different things, which leads to a powerful and violent conflict.

As Eastwood is about to execute Hackman, the latter holds up his hands and says, basically, "You can't kill me. I'm building a house." In other words, *I'm not the bad guy*. And from his standpoint, he's not. He's not evil or crazy or any other shorthand motivation. But there is inherent conflict between the sheriff and the former gunslinger that has come to town to punish the two men the law treated too gingerly. And that creates dramatic conflict and a powerful premise.

The Power of Tension

Just as mysteries are not only for mystery novels and suspense is not just for works of suspense, tension should infuse every page of every story. Tension is what keeps readers turning the pages. Sometimes people describe tension as a lesser form of suspense, but I think it's something different altogether and something writers must instill in their work, starting with the premise. Tension is the continuing feeling of unease, of things not being right in the world. But tension will not happen by accident. Tension comes because you have chosen the characters and conflicts with care. Tension must be baked into the premise.

Tension comes from the conflicting emotions that arise from inherent conflict.

Anytime you're tempted to put a book down without finishing it, you know the author has not injected enough tension into the premise. There's no emotional content underlying the action. There must be an emotional layer to make readers care. You must ask yourself what you character is thinking—then find a way to make that evident to the reader.

Got your emotional underpinning? What if there was not just one underlying emotional layer, but two (or more)—and those layered emotions conflicted with one another?

Now you've got serious tension.

Conflict always involves characters that want different things. That's not what I'm discussing here. This is about a single character fueled by conflicting emotions. Which happens all the time in real life, so why should we be surprised when it makes a novel so much more gripping?

You know that anytime you write a scene you should write it from a character's viewpoint. That means getting readers inside the character's head and letting them experience these events as the character does. That means you must understand the character's emotional state, how they are affected by what happens. But all too often writers pick a single emotion and stop. Don't make that mistake. Next time you write a scene—dig deeper. Don't stop at the superficial epidermal layer. Penetrate the skin.

First, think what the character's primary emotion or reaction will be. Then add another dimension. Is any situation completely happy? Or completely sad? Aren't most of the complicated situations in our complicated lives more complicated? Two emotions in conflict with one another make for more powerful storytelling.

Let's say your protagonist attends her father's funeral. Of course she's sad. She's lost the man who's been in her life since the day she was born, the only father she's ever known. She delivers a eulogy that rips hearts in two.

But a voice inside her is also thinking, Thank God that disapproving bastard is finally out of my life.

That's tension. That's conflicting emotion. And I might also add, that does not necessarily make your protagonist a bad person. It makes her more human.

Let's reimagine the story of the prodigal son in modern times. Two brothers, two years apart. One of them is loyal to the parents, hardworking, probably took over the family business. No one knew what happened to the other brother. He took off, did what he wanted, had all the adventures the first brother dreamed about but never achieved. They don't hear from him for years and start to worry that he might be dead.

And then one day without warning the other brother returns. He's well and was never in danger, just irresponsible and didn't give a thought to the fact that his family might be worried. When our protagonist sees his only brother again for the first time in decades, of course he rushes to embrace him. He loves his brother. So his primary emotion is one of joy and relief.

But as he holds his brother tight, he's also thinking: I wish you'd stayed dead, you selfish son-of-a bitch.

And while your reader is reeling, experiencing this honest human resentment that their father is treating the wayward brother as well or better than he did the loyal son who stayed at home, we go back into our protagonist's mind for a little more internal narrative. He's still thinking about his long-lost brother, but now he's thinking:

And now that my brother is back—what if he reveals my secret?

See what I mean? Conflicting emotions enrich a scene by deepening the conflict. Build it into the premise. Don't be satisfied by just letting your characters experience one obvious emotion. Give them more depth—depth that arises from the inherent conflicts among and between them. Instead of a resolute hero acting with complete certainty, have your character think, "I shouldn't do this, but I must." Or "I can't stop myself, but I know I'll pay for this later." That's the kind of tension readers love.

Talking Tension

Remember to instill tension in all your dialogue passages. *Dynamic Dialogue* discusses the importance of "off-the-nose" dialogue and allowing readers to read between the lines. Don't let a conversation simply be an exchange of information. When that goes on too long, it starts to seem like an infodump, that is, a way of feeding plot details to the reader. Even if some of that must take place, the passage will be much easier to read if the reader feels the tension between the characters while it's taking place. True tension is more about what *isn't* being said than what is. The primary emotion may relate to the exchange of information—but what dark undercurrents roil beneath the surface? Perhaps during the conversation in which the prodigal son explains where he's been all these years, the subtext suggests that one brother is actually collecting information to use against his brother at a later date. Perhaps his phrasing suggests hostility. "I suppose you'll want the last slice of cake. Might as well eat well while you can."

True tension does not arise from what is said. It arises from what is left unsaid.

Emotional friction will make any scene more dynamic and will make your inherent conflict, built into the premise, more intense. Competing egos, status struggles, clashes of styles and personalities—this is the stuff conflict thrives upon. Are the two professors really working together to make the program succeed, or is one trying to undermine the other? Someone said, "Academic politics are the worst, because the stakes are so small," but it must not seem small to the people involved. In team-up comics, Superman and Batman originally were great chums, but in the twenty-first century they are usually portrayed as having a hostile relationship because their methods, worldviews, and backgrounds are so different. Or because writers realize that conflicts make for better stories than chums.

One word about interior monologue: Don't be afraid of it. The age-old writing maxim, Show, don't tell, is a good rule of thumb, but it has also caused some aspiring writers to avoid interior monologue, that is, passages in which the characters effectively talk to themselves. Perhaps that seems too much like telling. But interior monologue can be your friend. Used wisely and sparingly, it can illuminate the characters and their emotional states, and can also create tension, maintaining your inherent conflict.

Like anything else, if you overuse interior monologue, it will start to seem clumsy. But you can use it to nudge your readers in the right direction. The brother in our earlier example can be thinking to himself, *Why does he always avert his eyes when he mentions our mother?* That's a nudge. Telling would be: *Ohmigosh, he killed Mom!* Or perhaps more subtly, *He can pretend he feels no guilt about what he's done, but I know that he does.* A subtle nudge planting an idea in the reader's head, or giving them some indication of the character's emotional state, can enhance a scene without descending to the level of telling.

There are some instances when interior monologue is not appropriate. Don't use it to tell the reader what they already know (or should not know). That will be just as trying as any other form of repetition. Readers want the story to move forward, not to run in place. Don't use interior monologue to restate or to hint at emotions that are obvious. Instead, use it to hint at those conflicting, multi-layered emotions hidden beneath the surface. Use it to suggest the far more interesting dichotomy between what is obvious and what is not.

And if you're wondering if you must put these interior digressions in italics, the answer is no. You can if you want. I think it gets annoying after a while, though if you've got that much monologue, it's may be time to scale it back. If you write the scene and the interior monologue correctly, from the viewpoint of the character, no one will have trouble recognizing that it is interior monologue, whether it is printed in italics or not.

Well-handled tension can enhance any story, and in many cases, may be the difference between an indifferent read and a keenly memorable one. So take this into account when devising your premise. Sharply edged inherent conflict can be your ticket to a winning premise and a successful story.

Highlights

1) Readily recognizable conflict leads to an exciting premise.

2) Conflict should be built into the premise.

3) Agenda conflict makes a sharper premise than evil.

4) The strongest premise involves strong opposing forces that have understandable but conflicting desires.

5) Tension arises from the conflicting emotions that arise from inherent conflict.

6) True tension does not come from what is said. It comes from what is left unsaid.

Red Sneaker Exercises

1) What motivates your antagonist? If you haven't done so, get the Character Detail Sheet in the back of *Creating Character* and fill it out for the primary antagonist. Try to understand as much as you can about this character. After you've done that, see if you can enrich the agenda conflict. Don't rely on the words "evil," "greedy," or "crazy." Come up with a motivation that puts them at odds with your protagonist but still seems plausible and perhaps even sympathetic. Perhaps the conflict arises not so much from what the antagonist wants but what he is willing to do to get it.

2) What is the relationship between your main characters? This could be your protagonist and antagonist or your protagonist and friends, sidekicks, or co-workers. Is there inherent conflict? Are there generation gaps, competing interests, conflicting egos, conspiracies, cliques, etc.? Using the *Amazing Race* approach, can you infuse these relationships with inherent conflict?

3) Tension is sometimes one of the more difficult concepts for aspiring writers to grasp. Conflict and suspense typically have more to do with plot, but tension almost always arises from character emotions. How can you use conflicting internal emotions to layer your story? In *Hamlet*, the title character is so torn he is virtually paralyzed for most of the play. What conflicting emotions tear your protagonist apart?

4) Take a look at your outline. (If you don't have one yet, read *Story Structure*.) It should identify the main event in each scene. Now ask yourself a question that may not be in the outline: What is your protagonist's primary emotion in each scene? What is his attitude toward the events taking place in that scene? Got that? Now dig deeper. What are the secondary or even tertiary emotions in conflict with those primary emotions? Make notes that will remind you to layer complex conflicting emotions into the scene by employing interior monologue, off-the-nose dialogue, and similar strategic devices.

5) Your dialogue is probably full of information that can be safely and freely exchanged. What is *not* being said? What is deliberately left unspoken? How can you convey or at least hint at that without resorting to telling? Can you

make your dialogue more interesting by introducing the unexpected?

CHAPTER 6: IF YOU ONLY BELIEVE

One can be absolutely truthful and sincere even though admittedly the most outrageous liar. Fiction and invention are the very fabric of life.

Henry Miller

You are probably familiar with the term "suspension of disbelief." Every time a reader starts a work of fiction, they are predisposed to accept certain matters as real even though they know they are not. If the book has a first-person narrator, readers accept the idea of someone telling them the story in great detail. If it's a mystery series, they accept the convention that your amateur sleuth keeps stumbling over corpses. If it's a thriller, they may accept the notions that one hero does the work of twenty and that he alone stands between us and global destruction.

But these suspensions of disbelief do not always happen automatically. The writer usually has to work for them. And even when they do happen automatically, there are authorial choices that can wipe them away in the space of a sentence. That must be avoided. A premise that does not sound believable does not invite readers to read. But a premise that does sound believable—no matter how far-fetched it may actually be—can be the ticket to great success.

Successful suspension of disbelief is essential to every story.

If They Believe It, They Will Come

The novelist's goal is not to mirror real life, but rather, to make their work seem realistic, which is an altogether different matter. Similarly, the question you should be asking yourself as you hone your premise is not, Could this really happen? Who cares if it could really happen? How sad the world of literature would be if writers limited themselves to stories that could actually happen. That would eliminate all science fiction, all fantasy, most thrillers, most mysteries. There would be no more Edgar Allan Poe, no Ray Bradbury, no Neil Gaiman. The world of literature would be poorer as a result.

Yes, when you started writing, someone probably told you to "write what you know," and that's more or less good advice. But it doesn't mean you should only write about situations that have actually occurred in your lifetime. It means you should draw on your own experiences when formulating characters and motivations. Your past can help you make your characters more lifelike. But it doesn't mean you can only write about actual events—and this is a frequent early-writer mistake. After creating a protagonist that's just like themselves and sticking the character in a setting that's where they live, they limit the plot to experiences they've actually had. *Writers should never limit themselves.* For a writer, the only limit should be the limit of your imagination. And imagination can and should be unlimited.

The fundamental question for a writer is not "Could this really happen?" The fundamental question

is, "Could I make readers believe this could really happen?"

Believability is of critical importance. As soon as your reader starts thinking, Nah, I'm not buying this, they're halfway to putting the book down and doing something else. But there are techniques you can use to make even the most extraordinary and unlikely events believable—within the context of your fictional universe. Here's the first and most important of these guiding principles.

Readers are more likely to accept a premise that is appealing.

Pretend to be an agent for a moment. I'm going to pitch an idea to you. Let's pretend it's the early 1990s. On an island somewhere near Costa Rica someone is building an amusement park—with dinosaurs. I know, it seems incredible but just go with me for a minute. See, scientists have cloned dinosaurs from ancient DNA. And someone thought it would be a good idea to put these dinos in a big zoo so tourists could gawk at them. Except then something goes wrong and these big lizards get loose and *Shazam!*— it's a technothriller. Our heroes (including some small children) are on the run from the dinosaurs, trying to stay alive and to get everyone out before the dinos have them for lunch. Literally.

If you really had been an agent back in the early 1990s hearing this pitch, you might have thought, that's preposterous. But today, chances are you recognize this as the premise for *Jurassic Park*, which was not only the biggest book of the decade but also spawned a sequel, four movies (so far), a theme park attraction, and a host of merchandising. The premise is absolutely preposterous and couldn't happen in a thousand years. Nonetheless, Michael Crichton sold it. How?

Part of the success derives from how Crichton presented it. Even though the premise is as far-fetched as could be, he brushed the veneer of science all over it. Crichton was known to be knowledgeable on scientific matters and was thought to have a scientific background often tapped in his writing (in truth, he went to medical school, never practiced or finished a residency, and never worked in a scientific field, but never mind that). Crichton employed the fundamental principle of the Big Lie Approach, which is to surround the falsehood with unassailable facts, which makes it easier for the gullible to make the final incredible leap.

So how was this premise presented? How did this dino park come to be? See, sixty-five million years ago, give or take a few, a mosquito sucked blood from a dinosaur. Okay, that's possible. We all know mosquitos suck blood. That blood contained DNA. Okay, still good, all blood has DNA. The mosquito was trapped in amber, which preserved it and the blood. Still possible. Paleontologists dig up stuff trapped in amber all the time. Modern-day scientists find that ancient blood and use the DNA to clone a dinosaur. Okay, now we're pushing credulity a bit. But then again, we've all read about cloning. If they can make Dolly the Sheep, why not Dino the Dinosaur? And finally, the scientists use genetic engineering to convert that DNA from one dinosaur into clones of every dinosaur species imaginable. The book is a little vague on this step, but we've heard of genetic engineering and at this point, why not?

In other words, Crichton surrounded the Big Lie with a lot of actual facts, eventually building to the big imaginative leap, but in a careful additive manner that made it much easier to swallow. The acorn of truth makes us believe in mighty fictional. Careful attention to making a fictional world internally consistent is also important. Crichton carefully covers nagging questions such as, Why anyone would want to do this? and How are they paying for this? and, of course, Why would anyone sabotage the park while still in it?

But the most important factor here, one likely to cause you to overlook any flaws, is that the idea of a dinosaur park, even if dangerous, is fun and attractive. Desirable. Original.

Who wouldn't go to a park that had live dinosaurs? I know I would. I don't care if they get loose, I'd be on the first flight out. People, particularly young people, have always been fascinated by dinosaurs—hence their frequent appearance in children's stories and tv shows and DisneyWorld. Crichton came to this idea when searching for an original premise. How? He basically combined his son's interest in dinosaurs with the concept behind a film he'd directed called *Westworld*, and Jurassic Park was born.

An appealing premise will leave readers *wanting* to believe in it.

That doesn't eliminate your need to create a convincing world, but it does make your work easier. If your premise has a seven-year old boy wake up one morning to find he's been turned into a platypus and now must travel to Skartoris to find a dirty sock, you may have trouble selling the book. Granted, it's original, but who cares? Who wants to go there? There is nothing appealing about the character, the quest, or the world of the adventure. You want a premise that will make nine out of ten people (including the agent getting the pitch) say, Yeah, I want to spend some time in that world.

WILLIAM BERNHARDT

Imagining the Unknown

Let's try another example, this time a fictional world that seems a lot less fun. Let's discuss Panem, the fictional futuristic setting of the blockbuster series I mentioned earlier, *The Hunger Games*.

Suzanne Collins is too savvy to slow the book down with a lot of exposition that is probably better left to the imagination, but here's what we know about this world. Sometime in our future, a devastating probably nuclear war occurred, killing millions of people and leaving civilization largely in ruins. We don't know when this happened, but it can't be too far in the future, because although the surviving technology is better than ours, it's not *that* much better than ours. A new civilization emerged from the ashes, one divided into districts, each district sharply stratified by class and economics. The Capitol is where the wealthy and the elite live. Districts 12 and 13 are filled with minorities and coal miners and others on the bottom rung of the social hierarchy. To unify this civilization and prevent unrest, the Capitol holds annual games in which representatives of each district send randomly chosen teenagers to fight to the death—while everyone else watches on television.

Why would any reader believe in this dystopian world? For that matter, why would any reader want to believe in this dystopian world?

For anyone with any knowledge of politics or history, this world seems all too credible. Virtually all societies have been marked by class stratifications, whether they are overt, as in the UK, or somewhat less so, as in the US. (But every time you hear a politician talk about a "middle-class tax cut," you know the stratifications still exist.) For a historian, there is nothing new about a totalitarian government arising from the ashes of a devastating conflict. And the most bizarre element, the hunger games, is far from unprecedented. There is nothing new about the idea of "bread and circuses," blood sport offered as entertainment to the masses to keep them amused and distracted, and also as a not-so-subtle warning about the fate of those who might challenge the powers that be.

This concept goes back at least to the Roman Empire and probably much further. Violent sports have been a hallmark of almost every Western civilization. Even today, huge numbers flock to stadiums to watch brutal athletic competitions. Why has football become the most popular sport in America? Is it the most complex sport? The most athletically challenging? Does it require the most skill? Probably not, but it is certainly the most brutal. (Soccer and rugby fans may dispute this, but there are relatively few cases of early-onset brain damage in those sports, while it has become distressingly commonplace for graduates of the NFL.) People from all walks of life seem to have an exciting, cathartic experience watching big guys bash their heads together. Mix that reality with the popularity of television competitions like *Survivor*, and then ask yourself if the hunger games are all that hard to believe.

The world of Panem is appealing, but in a different way than Jurassic Park. It's not that we'd all love to go there. It's that it makes sense. It seems internally consistent. More, it seems like something that might arise out of a nuclear conflict. It has political and historic antecedents. As a result, it gave Collins not only a framework for telling a terrific story, but also for making sharp observations about politics and entertainment and the inevitable results of a sharply stratified society. If you've read the third and final volume (and I won't spoil the secrets here), then you've been treated to what can only be seen as Collins's own views about the inevitable result of a stratified society as well as the viability of violent rebellion, even in service of a sympathetic cause. Collins avoids the obvious Disneyfied happy endings that most readers probably expected in favor of tragedy and disillusionment, forcing readers, even in the context of a fantasy novel, to seriously confront the difficult issues addressed.

When you create your premise, you must propose a credible setting. That may be harder for works of science fiction and fantasy like those I've discussed, but then again, I've read books set in real cities that still didn't seem authentic. Believability is something that must be earned, by careful painstaking contemplation and writing, bearing in mind that the more truths you can surround your world with, be they scientific, historical, political, or otherwise, the more real your world will become. When readers see elements they recognize, they are more likely to find your premise intriguing. You want them to understand that reading your book will take them to a unique, original, appealing world they have not visited before.

POWERFUL PREMISE

Highlights

1) Successful suspension of disbelief is essential to every story.

2) The fundamental question for a writer is not "Could this really happen?" The fundamental question is, "Could I make readers believe this could really happen?"

3) Readers are more likely to accept a premise that is appealing.

4) An appealing premise will leave readers *wanting* to believe in it.

Red Sneaker Exercises

1) Michael Crichton's idea for *Jurassic Park* came from paying attention to the pervasive interest that some people (particularly young people) had in dinosaurs. Is there another interest that you could use as the core idea for an ingenious and appealing original premise? What has always fascinated you? What do your children love? What have you spent most of your non-essential spending on?

2) Could your premise be expanded to be bolder, more daring, more original? If your characters are simply people you know, in settings you know, having experiences you've had, will that be enough? Expand on the ordinary. Is it possible you could transform your premise into something more original, more exciting, more likely to grab the attention of a literary agent or a reader?

3) Do you have a high-concept, larger-than-life idea at the core of your story? If so, how will you make it believable to your readers? How will you make it appealing? Are you creating a world that will intrigue readers (like *The Hunger Games*)? Are you creating a world readers will want to visit (like *Jurassic Park*)?

4) Perhaps the situations your protagonist will experience take a farther journey from everyday life than the usual. How will you sell this to the reader? How will you convince them this could actually happen? Can you use the Big Lie technique? What grains of truth can you seed to build your world? What well known realities could form the basis for your larger-than-life construction?

CHAPTER 7: PITCHING

Life shrinks or expands in proportion to one's courage.

Anais Nin

In this final chapter, let's discuss what you will do with this superb premise you've devised. First, you're going to write a wonderful book based upon that brilliant premise, but after that, you're going to get others interested in your book. That brings you to pitching, the process of trying to get a literary agent or editor interested in your work.

At almost every writer's conference I've ever attended, someone has spoken on the subject of pitching—all too often, someone who has never done it. I've organized a writers' conference for many years now. Every year I talk to my agents to find out what they want, what works and what doesn't. So here's where I take this discussion of premise out of the theoretical and into the practical.

One Minute or Less

Three sentences should be enough. That may seem too simple, but it's true. And that doesn't mean you shouldn't be prepared to talk at greater length about your brilliant idea. But if you haven't grabbed the agent's attention in three sentences, you probably never will.

You should be able to explain your premise well in three sentences.

At many writer events, you will never have the opportunity to gab at great length. Some conferences, particularly the large New York affairs, give people sadly brief periods of time to interact with their agents. This is a simple reality of large conferences that attract many people. If you're hunting an agent, instead of finding the biggest conference or the one with the most agents, it may be wiser to seek the conference where you will have more time with more people. A pitch is always a speed date, but some speed dates are better than others, based upon a combination of who you're dating and the environment. Often the largest conferences result in the fewest manuscript acquisitions, because the agents don't have the time or inclination to take anyone seriously.

Regardless of how much time you're allotted, you should be able to explain your fundamental premise efficiently. If time permits and the agent is interested, you can go into more detail or answer questions. But a minute should be enough to explain the premise. Remember the core elements of great stories. Make sure your pitch includes a discussion of the main character, the setting, and the basic plot.

Once that's established, establish all the other elements we've covered that make premises stronger. The originality, I hope, will speak for itself. Try to explain why your book is a clever variation on a theme without resorting to the cliché "One Successful Book Meets Another Successful Movie" formula. Equally cliché is the now timeworn "What if" question as a way of introducing your premise. You can do better—and you should, because you'll never capture agents' attention or convince them you're an original thinker by saying something they've already heard a hundred times. Instead come up with a fresh approach. And please don't swagger. "This book of mine will be the next...(fill in the blank with the latest stratospheric sales success)!" Overt references to successful books from the past are not necessary. If that agent is worth having, they're already well aware of what's been on the bestseller list. If there are legitimate connections between your project and some megahit, they'll be able to see it for themselves.

While we're on the subject of originality, let me mention some of the other preposterous attention-grabbing devices I've heard advocated, such as dressing up in funky costumes or assuming the persona of a character. This has nothing to do with the merits of your book, nor does it suggest any sort of literary excellence. Arguably, you've made yourself more memorable (in a good way?), but that's not enough. If your pitch succeeds, it will be based on the pitch itself, not your costume (or speaking in the character of your protagonist, or presenting a business card with your photo on it, or the candy or toy you brought, etc.). These gimmicks seem like cheap substitutes for literary originality, desperate attempts to obtain attention the pitch or book would never merit on their own. Last time I attended a big conference where the speaker on pitches (who eventually admitted he had never pitched in his life) advocated this sort of thing, I asked him to give me a single instance when these sorts of gimmicks had resulted in someone getting an agent or selling a book. He couldn't. So leave the gorilla suit at home.

Gimmicks won't sell your book. A strong premise, well explained, will.

Make sure you describe the high stakes. Why does this matter? What's your answer to the question, "Who cares?"

The same elements you devised to make your book more compelling to your reader will likely have the same effect on this agent. Don't make your story sound small. Make it sound big and important. I've heard pitches in which unpublished authors, perhaps out of timidity or lack of confidence, undersold their work. That's not a winning approach. Modesty will get you nothing in this arena. Your book is the biggest most important thing that's ever been written, or at least you should convince yourself of that before you try to sell it. If you can't convince yourself, how could you possibly convince anyone else?

Practice Makes Perfect

Don't be afraid to practice. The best pitches don't sound canned, but rehearsal might still help. Making it sound natural can be part of what you practice. You wouldn't play a basketball game or perform a piano piece without practicing, so why on earth would you do anything so important as pitching the book you've worked on for years without practicing? Watch yourself in the mirror as your present your pitch, or better yet, make a video. (Your cell phone has a video camera that will be just fine for this.) Do you seem friendly (no one wants to get into business with an unpleasant author)? Do you seem confident? Did you make eye contact? Did your hands distract from your pitch? Did you have energy? If you seemed bored by your pitch, everyone else will be bored, too.

If you saw this pitch, would you buy this book?
Practice your pitch before you deliver it.

POWERFUL PREMISE

Be Yourself. Everyone Else is Already Taken

I once asked a major editor at Putnam what he liked to see in a pitch. He told me he always tells people who come to see him: "Don't give me a pitch. I don't want a pitch. Just tell me about your book." I think he was saying he didn't want a performance. At that very conference, speakers were advising authors to open with a snazzy grabber, a paradox, a famous quote, or a phrase with lots of alliteration. (No, I am not making this up.) I think this editor was miffed, if not offended, that anyone thought anything so superficial could influence his purchasing decisions. He doesn't want you to sell your book like people sell deodorant on television. He's not a child and he's not attracted to sparkly shiny objects. He wants to hear about your book. Of course, you still want to give a terrific pitch. Just make sure the focus is your premise.

If it helps you to write out your pitch in advance, then by all means do it. But please do not read it during your meeting. Nothing could be duller than hearing a written proposal read aloud. Even the shyest author on earth ought to able to remember a minute's worth of information about the book they spent a year or more writing. If necessary, make notes. List a few talking points, things you want to make sure you cover. But don't get so distracted by the notes that you forget to look at the person you're addressing. In my own experience, I find that if I've prepared enough for a speech, I can usually deliver it without notes, but if I have notes in hand, I will constantly look at them even though I don't need to. Don't take anything with you that you don't need.

Don't perform, pitch.

Truth is, most of the fundamental principles of public speaking apply here, even though you aren't actually giving a speech as such. Be yourself. Make sure it sounds natural, not like a performance. And let your own personality shine through. If the agent likes you, if they see you have a winning smile, of course that makes them more likely to work with you. That's just human nature. Even Jacqueline Susann, the most successful author of her time, was fired by her editor because she was too unpleasant to work with. As Michael Korda described in his memoir, despite the fact that *Once Is Not Enough* was a huge hit, when she sent her next book proposal, he sent her a nice bouquet with a card that read, "For us, once was enough."

Regardless of how much time you get, remember that first impressions are typically made in about fifteen seconds. Even if your premise is intriguing, if you've already put the agent off, your chances are slender.

I don't think overt sucking up is necessary, but anything that shows you know who the agents are, that you're familiar with their work, can only be helpful. "I thought you might be interested in this because you also represent..." Even if it doesn't persuade on its own, it at least shows that you've done your homework, which means you're treating this seriously and professionally. You're not a dilettante. You're a professional who knows what they're doing. If the agent wants to fill time by allowing you to ask questions, then ask some. Show your interest. This is another opportunity to demonstrate that you've done your homework.

Be friendly. Let your personality shine through.

Miscellaneous Pitching Points

I always recommend that people shake hands with the agent they're meeting, on their way in and again on their way out. It may be a small thing, but tactile contact usually warms people up a little. Break the imaginary barriers. This may be particularly important for women, because some men were raised (particularly in the South) to not extend a hand to a woman, but to only take it if it is offered. So break the ice. Give the guy your hand. Often you'll be able to see the other person melt a little right then and there.

I have heard people advise authors not to reveal the ending of their story in the pitch. That's probably good general advice, but in a few cases, I've had students pitching stories in which the ending was part of what made it unique, or contributed to the genre twist. If that's true for your book—tell. If you've got something that will increase the agent's interest, spill. It's pointless to keep secrets that result in the book never being published.

By the same token, it is not necessary to fill the agent in on all the plot developments, subsidiary characters, subplots, or twists and turns along the way. They won't be able to absorb it all and will likely get lost in all the names and details. Focus on the big picture, the high concept. Present your premise in the way that makes it sound most interesting.

If you have some unique experiences or credentials that relate to your book, don't be afraid to reveal them, given an opportunity (not in lieu of describing your book). If you have any serious major prior publications, you can tell them that too, but if it's not on the national level, it's probably not going to help. The fact that you won third place in your writing club's annual contest isn't going to

2

matter, though the fact that you self-published a novel that hit the Kindle Top 10, or that you have two million Twitter followers, probably will.

Take a look at these pitches and see if you can tell which is more likely to be effective.

Pitch #1:

This novel is about a timid mousy girl in the deep South named Samantha who meets an outgoing pig farmer named Bob. They go through several meetings but never get together. In fact, they are separated for eight years due to various circumstances. But at the end, they come together and marry and make a happy future together.

Pitch #2:

Nineteen-year-old Samantha's life is turned upside down when a trolley car accident kills her mother and injures her, leaving her alone and living in the basement of the boy she's been crushing on since grade school. She thinks Bob doesn't know she's alive. He spends all his time with his pigs, but one event after another forces them together. They fall in love. Just as Bob is about to propose, the war separates them, but Samantha never loses faith that they will be reunited one day. The army puts Bob on the front lines, constantly in danger, and the failure of the farm makes all Samantha's friends urge her to marry the town banker, even though she doesn't love him.

Possibly neither of these pitches sends you running to the bookstore. But do you see how much difference a dynamic presentation can make? Both pitches concern the same book, but one uses vivid language, tangible detail, and references to high stakes to make it more appealing.

POWERFUL PREMISE

You will do the same next time you pitch. Show how excited you are about this book. And smile.

Highlights

1) You should be able to explain your premise well in three sentences.

2) Gimmicks won't sell your book. A strong premise, well explained, will.

3) Practice your pitch before you deliver it.

4) Don't perform, pitch.

5) Be friendly. Let your own personality shine through.

Red Sneaker Exercises

1) Write out a pitch that takes about one minute to deliver. Take the same care in this pitch that you would take with anything else of importance that you write, which means you'll go through several drafts, each time improving the content and the language. Make sure it contains all the great elements of great stories and great premises.

2) Practice your pitch in front of a mirror. Then make a video recording and watch the playback. Do you seem natural? Are you friendly? Relaxed? Are you able to deliver the pitch without excessive recourse to notes? When you've gotten to the point that you're reasonably pleased with it, get a friend to pretend to be the agent. Smile, shake their hand, and deliver your pitch. Maybe you can even answer some unscripted questions. Then let your friend give you

some feedback. If you've put in enough practice, you'll be pleased with the results.

APPENDIX A: PREMISE WORKSHEET

Working Title:

_____

Word count:

_____

Viewpoint Character:

_____

Setting:

_____

Basic Plot:

_____

What makes it unique:

_____

_____

High Stakes:

_____

_____

WILLIAM BERNHARDT

Describe the premise in three sentences or less:

_____
_____
_____
_____
_____
_____
_____

Describe your story in one minute (probably around 200 words):

_____
_____
_____
_____
_____
_____

Not satisfied yet? Raise the stakes.

How could the public stakes get worse?

_____
_____
_____
_____

POWERFUL PREMISE

How could the personal stakes matter more?

_____

_____

_____

_____

APPENDIX B: PITCHING DOs and DON'Ts

Do:

Prepare and practice
Be natural
Let your personality shine through
Be friendly
Smile
Shake hands
Show enthusiasm
Make your books sound terrific
Cover all the elements of great stories
Explain what makes your book unique
Dramatize the high stakes
Be able to explain the premise well in one minute
Mention any credentials relevant to the book
Mention significant prior publishing experience
Mention your author platform (if you have one)

Don't:

Rely on silly gimmicks
Dress up or act funny
Talk about how nervous you are (they already know)
Put on a show
Give the agent anything (unless asked)
Make a negative impression

Compare your books to other books (unless appropriate)
Compare yourself to other writers
Get lost in the details
Take too long to get the premise across
Pitch a novel you haven't finished yet
Swagger
Pitch to an agent without checking their credentials
Pitch to an agent you wouldn't want

APPENDIX C: SYNOPSIS

Some agents may request a synopsis at a pitch session or with a written query letter. The most difficult part of writing a synopsis is trying to get the essential details of your story down to a page or so without making it completely boring. Don't be discouraged if you don't get it right the first time. Or the tenth. Writing a good synopsis can be extremely challenging.

Agents (and editors) differ in their requirements, but generally they will ask for a synopsis in one or two pages, single-spaced. These people are busy, so if you can do it well in one page, you should.

Generally speaking, a good synopsis will follow the chronological order of the story and will be composed of three elements:

1) Identify your protagonist, primary conflict, and setting. Agents are always looking for something different, particularly a fresh point of view. Focus on how can you make your story *not* sound like every other book of this type.

2) Convey any major plot turns, conflicts and characters so your summary will make sense to whoever reads it. Basically, it should describe the narrative arc of the book. Make sure you explain the protagonist's actions and

motivations in a way that makes sense and doesn't sound cliché. But don't get so swept up in telling the details that you forget to describe the emotions your characters experience. Human emotion is what makes a story powerful.

3) In the final section, indicate how the major conflicts are resolved. Yes, give away the ending and any major surprises. The synopsis should be a clear presentation of your novel that doesn't leave the reader confused. You aren't likely to sell your book by leaving out the best parts.

Please remember: agents are looking for people who can write well. If your synopsis doesn't shine, why would anyone look at your manuscript? Focus on clarity, precision, and concision. You don't have enough space to waste words.

Avoid the primary mistakes aspiring writers make when writing synopses:

1) Don't try to cram in too many characters and plot details. Focus on what is necessary to understand the narrative arc. Eliminate unnecessary details, descriptions, and backstory.

2) Avoid "writerly" writing. Just tell the story. In other words, no genre jargon, no references to other books, no creative-writing-class terms of art. Don't say, "In a flashback, Aura sees that..." Don't say, "This is a coming-of-age story in which..."

3) Don't try to inject emotion or excitement into your synopsis with adverbs or clichés. I understand it's difficult to convey the emotional content of the story in so few words. Do the best you can. But don't resort to saying, "In a poignant scene, Aura…" or "In a hilarious moment of mistaken identity…" Your story must speak for itself, even in the synopsis.

4) Don't make the mistake of writing back cover copy instead of a synopsis. This is not the time to use generalizations or hyperbole. A good opening tagline might be an effective teaser, but don't write the whole synopsis that way.

APPENDIX D: SHOWING vs. TELLING

Aspiring writers are often confused by the adage, "Show, don't tell." After all, there are times when you have to tell the readers stuff (like, what happens next). Usually this adage refers to matters that are internal or invisible, matters contained within a character's heart. Is internal monologue telling? (Perhaps) Is backstory telling? (Yes, but it may be unavoidable). How can you make sure the reader gets something if you don't tell them?

The most important time to avoid telling is when you're conveying your character's emotional state or motivation. Sometimes characterization, that is, external character details, can suggest character information. Sometimes a well-written descriptive passage can cue the reader to the character's emotional state.

Here's a basic approach for showing information without telling, while still ensuring any attentive reader will get it. This is all based on one fundamental principle: **The difference between showing and telling is the difference between presenting visible facts and invisible facts.**

1) Determine what it is you want your reader to understand. Don't write it out as such in your story. But ask yourself: How will this influence the character's actions?

2)   Look for a scene in your story where this invisible fact is relevant. (If you can't find one, create one.) How can you tip off the reader by showing this fact influencing your character's actions in this scene?

3)   Consider other contributing factors. The character's personality, the situation, and this invisible fact combine (conspire?) to influence the character's actions. Make them produce something visible—a choice, a consequence, a reaction. How will these invisible facts reveal themselves?

4)   Write down the visible part—the choice, consequence, or reaction.

5)   Reread the scene. Have you given your reader enough information to glean the invisible fact? If they "get it for themselves," it will have a greater impact.

APPENDIX E: THE WRITER'S CALENDAR

Okay, you've got a powerful premise. Now what? How do you turn that premise into a book?

By starting today, and working every day until the job is finished. Is it possible to finish a top-quality manuscript in six months? It is if you're willing to do the work necessary to make it happen. Here's how you do it.

Week 1
Commit to your writing schedule.
Find your studio.
Sign the Writer's Contract in Appendix E. Inform friends and family.
Think about what you want to write. Start thinking like a writer.

Week 2
Commit to a premise—then make it bigger. Is it big and unique enough to attract a publisher?
Commit to a genre. What's your spin on the genre? How will you make it the same—but different? Research as needed.

Week 3
Develop your main protagonist and antagonist.
Complete job applications/bio (in Appendix A) for both. What are their best qualities—and worst? What drives them?

What is your protagonist's character arc? What does he/she want, seek, desire?

Write a half-page example of dialogue for each major character in their distinct voice.

Week 4

Put all major events (scenes) on index cards, approximately sixty total, as described in *Story Structure*.

Arrange cards by acts. Highlight the Plot Turning Points and Character Turning Points.

Type the index cards into an outline, adding detail when you have it.

Week 5

Think about the shape of your story—the Plot. Will your character experience positive growth or maturation? Redemption? Disillusionment?

Map out twists and turns to maintain reader interest. What is the last thing the reader will suspect?

Don't shy away from a great scene because it doesn't fit your story as you currently understand it. See if you can change the story to accommodate the great scene.

Weeks 6-18

Write at least five pages every day—ten on Saturdays. No editing. Just keep moving ahead.

Do additional writing as necessary to complete 10 % of the book each week.

Week 19-21

Perform triage on what you've written. Revise. Then revise

more. Reference the Revision lecture on the Fundamentals of Fiction DVD to spot potential problems.

Week 22-24

Give the manuscript to trusted reader(s).

Reread it yourself, focusing on character consistency, character depth. Are the characters sympathetic or empathetic?

Reread it focusing on plot, pacing, story logic, theme. Is the story plausible? Obtain comments from readers. Incorporate comments from readers where appropriate.

Reread it focusing on dialogue.

Set it aside, then reread it with fresh eyes. Do you see problems you didn't spot before?

And then—

Bounce your ideas off friends, agents, and editors. If people don't ask to see your manuscript, your premise needs work. If people ask to see pages but don't take you on, your manuscript needs work. Consider attending a small-group writing seminar to give your book that final push it needs to be publishable.

APPENDIX F: COMMONLY CONFUSED WORDS

Affect/Effect: Contrary to the commonly espoused rule, both words can be used as nouns and verbs, depending upon your meaning. *Affect* is usually a verb meaning "to have an effect on," but it can also be used to mean "countenance" or "emotion," as in, "The Vulcan had a flat affect." *Effect* is usually a noun meaning "impact" or "consequence," but it can also be used as a verb (a shortened form of "effectuate") meaning "to bring about."

Aggravate/Irritate: *Aggravate* means to worsen. *Irritate* means to inflame or anger. Many people use *aggravate* to mean "vex, annoy, or irritate," but that is not strictly speaking correct.

Allude/Refer: Yes, there is a difference. To *allude* is "to hint at or mention indirectly." To *refer* is "to mention directly." "Are you alluding to my height when you call me 'Napoleon?'" "You're short," she said, referring to his height.

Alternate/Alternative: *Alternate* means "one after the other." *Alternative* means "one instead of the other." Walking requires the *alternate* use of the left and right foot. The *alternative* is the bus.

Amused/Bemused: *Amused* means you're having a good time. *Bemused* means you're befuddled or puzzled or deep in thought.

Attorney General/Attorneys General: The plural of *attorney general* is *attorneys general*, as in: "Several assistant attorneys general appeared on behalf of the state." In this phrase, *general* is an adjective following the noun (a postpositive adjective), not a noun. The same is true of "Presidents Elect" or "mothers-in-law" or "passersby," but is not correct for a true compound word such as "spoonful." The plural would be "spoonfuls," not "spoonsful."

Besides/Beside*: Besides* means other than or in addition. *Beside* means alongside. "No one *besides* her son could stand so close beside her."

Big of a/Big of: As always, eliminate unnecessary words that add nothing to the sentence. Don't say, "How *big of a* case is it?" The same is true of "long of a" "slow of a" and other similar constructions.

Childlike/Childish*: Childish* is a pejorative adjective suggesting that someone is acting like a child and that isn't good. The positive way of saying the exact same thing is *childlike*.

Complement/Compliment: To *complement* is to complete or pair with or round out. To *compliment* is to praise.

Continuous/Continual*: Continuous* means uninterrupted.

POWERFUL PREMISE

Continual means repeated, but intermittent. "Jack had to wind the grandfather clock continually to make it run continuously."

Convince/Persuade: You *convince* someone of something, but you *persuade* them to do something. *Convince* is usually followed by "that" or "of," but *persuade* is always followed by "to."

Corroborate/Collaborate*:* To *corroborate* evidence is to fortify it with additional evidence. To *collaborate* on a project is to work with someone else on it.

Could/Couldn't Care Less*:* If your intent is to say that you care as little as it is possible to care, use the phrase "couldn't care less." If you could care less, that means you already care at least a little.

Counsel/Council*:* *Counsel* means "advice," but it can also be a noun meaning "lawyer" or "consultant," in effect, a shortened form of "counselor." *Council* is a committee that leads or governs.

Credulous/Incredible*:* The *incredible* is unbelievable. Credulous people are gullible. *Incredulous* means you do not believe.

Datum/Data*:* *Datum* is the traditional singular, *data* the plural, but today, many people use *data* as a singular noun and few dictionaries or grammarians are still suggesting that it is incorrect.

Deserts/Desserts*:* In this example: What one deserves is one's *just deserts*. This use of *deserts* is related to the verb *deserve*. "The unsuccessful plaintiff got his just deserts." Deserts are dry, arid, sandy places, preferably in Cabo, and desserts include tiramisu and sopaipillas.

Discreet/Discrete: *Discreet* means "careful" or "prudent." *Discrete* means "separate, distinct, or unconnected." "Jack was *discreet* about his secret for maintaining two wives and two *discrete* households."

Disinterested/Uninterested*:* *Disinterested* means impartial or fair. *Uninterested* means not interested, bored, unengaged. "The judge was disinterested in the outcome of the case, and uninterested in the uncivil behavior of the divorce attorney."

Divorcé/Divorcée*:* *Divorcé* is for men, *divorcée* is for women.

Elicit/Illicit: To *elicit* is to evoke. *Illicit* means "illegal."

Emigrate/Immigrate: It's all about coming and going. You *emigrate* from a country and *immigrate* to another. For a mnemonic, remember that "exit" starts with an "e," like "*emigrate*," and "in" starts with an "i," like "*immigrate*."

Eminent/Imminent/Immanent: *Eminent* means "famous or superior." *Imminent* means "impending." *Immanent* (rare these days, outside of the church) means "inherent or dwelling within."

POWERFUL PREMISE

Farther/Further: *Farther* refers to physical distance. *Further* means "to a greater extent or degree."

Fewer/Less: "Fewer" is used when the items in question can be counted. "Less" is used for items not subject to easy enumeration. "We had *fewer* writers than we'd hoped for, but *less* optimism than I expected." Obviously, the sign in every supermarket reading "Ten Items or Less" is just wrong.

Hadn't/Hadn't of: *"Hadn't of"* is ugly and grammatically incorrect.

Hanged/Hung: Murderers and horse thieves used to be *hanged*. "Hung" is incorrect in that context. But paintings and coats are *hung*.

Historic/Historical: *Historic* means "having a place in history." *Historical* means "pertaining to the subject of history."

Home in/Hone in: "We need to *home* in on the precise problem."

Imply/Infer: To imply means to suggest something. To infer means to conclude from available evidence. Speakers imply. Listeners infer. Writers imply. Readers infer. "You imply that I'm a moron," the husband said. "You infer correctly," the wife replied.

Ingenuous/Ingenious: *Ingenuous* means naïve, frank, or candid, coming from the same root word as "ingénue."

Ingenious means crafty. Disingenuous means dishonest.

It's/Its*: It's* is the contraction for *it is. Its* is a possessive pronoun.

Jones's/Joneses*:* One guy is a *Jones*, but the whole family are the *Joneses*. If you are discussing something they own, that would be the *Joneses'*. The same is true of other family names ending in "s."

Laudable/Laudatory*: Laudable* means praiseworthy. *Laudatory* means praiseful. "He did a laudable job of reading the laudatory psalms."

Lie/Lay*: Lie* means to recline. The simple past tense of *lie* is *lay* and the past participle is *lain*. Lay can also be a verb indicating placement, and therein lies the confusion. The past tense of *lay* is *laid*. "Today you *lie* in the same bed where I lay my car keys."

Memoranda/Memorandum*: Memoranda* is plural, *memorandum* is singular.

Neither/Nor*:* Whether the verb in a "neither/nor" sentence is singular or plural depends upon the second element. Therefore, "Neither you nor I *am* responsible," but, "Neither I nor they *are* responsible." "Neither" by itself means by implication "neither one," so it takes a singular verb, as in, "Neither of your objections *is* correct." The same is true for "either," as in: "Either the plaintiff or one of the other lawyers *is* responsible for the judge's verdict."

Number/Amounts: Countable items have a *number*. Non-countable items are measured in *amounts*.

Overflowed/Overflow: *Overflowed* is the past tense and past participle of the verb *overflow*.

Persecute/Prosecute: To *persecute* is to torment. To *prosecute* is to conduct criminal proceedings. "The defendant felt *persecuted* when the DA *prosecuted* him the second time."

Principal/Principle: P*rincipal* means "main or primary." *Principle* means "rule or standard." "The school principal said his principal goal was to reinvest the trust fund principal, as a matter of principle."

Prophesy/Prophecy: *Prophesy* is a verb meaning "to foretell." P*rophecy* is a noun indicating what was foretold. "Madame Martel dropped her fee per prophecy, because she could prophesy a downturn in the economy."

Prospective/Perspective: *Prospective* means "potential." *Perspective* means "viewpoint."

Ravage/Ravish: A famous headline in a Minnesota newspaper read: "Queen Elizabeth Ravished." As you might have guessed, the ocean liner *Queen Elizabeth* caught fire and burned, and the paper should have said "Queen Elizabeth Ravaged" (though that sill doesn't sound very good). *Ravaged* means "damaged or destroyed." *Ravished* means "carried away (by force or by emotion) or sexually assaulted." When you say that your sweetheart looked *ravishing*, you're not implying a desire to do anything illegal. You're saying the sight of her swept you away with emotion.

Regardless/Irregardless: *Irregardless* is still considered substandard by most authorities, though it technically has the same meaning as "regardless."

Regretful/Regrettable: *Regretful* means "full of regret." *Regrettable* means "unfortunate, a cause for regret." "Florence *regretfully* swept up the pieces of the Ming vase she had *regrettably* smashed."

Reigned/Reined: "The legal fees when Queen Elizabeth reigned had to be *reined* in by the Privy Council."

Reluctant/Reticent: Although people often use these as synonyms, their true meanings aren't even similar. *Reluctant* means unwilling, but *reticent* means silent. "The *reluctant* witness was *reticent* on the witness stand."

Stationer/Stationery/Stationary: A *stationer* sells *stationery* (a good mnemonic device is to recall that there is an *"er"* in *"paper"*). S*tationary* objects (like stationery) do not move.

Stolen/Robbed: Money and other things of value are *stolen*. People, places, and businesses are *robbed*.

Therefore/Therefor: *Therefore* means "accordingly" or "in conclusion." *Therefor* is an ugly and archaic piece of legalese meaning "for it" or "for them," as in, "He bought a bicycle and paid *therefor*."

Tortuous/Torturous: *Tortuous* means "winding or crooked or twisty." *Torturous* means "painful." "During the tortuous drive, Jack developed a torturous ache in his backside."

Who/Whom: Most modern grammarians now say "who" can always be used in place of "whom" at the beginning of a sentence or clause. "Whom" should still be used after a preposition. So "Who from?" is correct, but so is "From whom?" Most American lexicographers, from Daniel Webster on down, have argued for clarifying the confusion by eliminating "whom" altogether, but it hasn't happened yet.

Whose/Who's: *Whose* is the possessive relative pronoun. *Who's* is the contraction for *who is*. "*Who's* the person for *whose* benefit the trust fund was established?"

APPENDIX G: THE WRITER'S READING LIST

The Chicago Manual of Style. 16th ed. Chicago: University of Chicago Press, 2010.

Cook, Vivian. *All in a Word: 100 Delightful Excursions into the Uses and Abuses of Words.* Brooklyn: Melville House, 2010.

Fowler, H.W. *Fowler's Modern English Usage.* 3rd ed. Rev. Ernest Gowers. N.Y. & Oxford: Oxford University Press, 2004.

Goldman, William. *Adventures in the Screen Trade: A Personal View of Hollywood and Screenwriting.* New York: Grand Central, 1989.

Hale, Constance. *Sin and Syntax: How to Create Wickedly Effective Prose.* New York: Broadway Books, 2001.

Hart, Jack. *A Writer's Coach: The Complete Guide to Writing Strategies That Work.* New York: Anchor Books, 2006.

Jones, Catherine Ann. *The Way of Story: The Craft and Soul of Writing.* Studio City: Michael Wiese Productions, 2007.

Klauser, Henriette Anne. *Writing on Both Sides of the Brain*. San Francisco: Harper & Row, 1987.

Maass, Donald. *The Fire in Fiction: Passion, Purpose, and Techniques to Make Your Novel Great*. Cincinnati: Writers Digest Books, 2009.

Maass, Donald. *Writing the Breakout Novel: Insider Advice for Taking Your Fiction to the Next Level*. Cincinnati: Writers Digest Books, 2001.

Maass, Donald. *Writing 21st Century Fiction: High Impact Techniques for Exceptional Storytelling*. Cincinnati: Writers Digest Books, 2012.

O'Conner, Patricia T. *Woe Is I: The Grammarphobe's Guide to Better English in Plain English*. 2nd ed. New York: Riverhead Books, 2003.

O'Conner, Patricia T. *Origins of the Specious: Myths and Misconceptions of the English Language*. New York: Random House, 2009.

Strunk, William, Jr., and White, E.B. *The Elements of Style*. 4th ed. N.Y.: Macmillan, 2000.

Truss, Lynne. *Eats Shoots & Leaves: The Zero Tolerance Guide to Punctuation*. New York: Gotham Books, 2005.

Vogler, Christopher. *The Writer's Journey: Mythic Structure for Storytellers and Screenwriters*. Studio City: Michael Wiese Productions, 1992.

POWERFUL PREMISE

Zinsler, William. *On Writing Well: The Classic Guide to Writing Nonfiction.* 30th Anniv. Ed. New York: Harper Perennial, 2006.

About the Author

William Bernhardt is the bestselling author of more than thirty books, including *The Game Master*, the blockbuster Ben Kincaid series, a poetry book (*The White Bird*), and *Nemesis: The Final Case of Eliot Ness*, which is currently in development for an NBC miniseries. In addition, Bernhardt founded the Red Sneaker Writing Center, hosting writing workshops and small-group seminars and becoming one of the most in-demand writing instructors in the nation. His programs have educated many authors now published at major New York houses.

Bernhardt holds a Masters Degree in English Literature and is the only writer to have received the Southern Writers Guild's Gold Medal Award, the Royden B. Davis Distinguished Author Award (University of Pennsylvania) and the H. Louise Cobb Distinguished Author Award (Oklahoma State), which is given "in recognition of an outstanding body of work that has profoundly influenced the way in which we understand ourselves and American society at large." In addition to the novels, he has written plays, including a musical (book and music), humor, nonfiction books, children's books, biography, and *New York Times* crossword puzzles. OSU dubbed him "Oklahoma's Renaissance Man," noting that in addition to producing novels, he can "write a sonnet, play a sonata, plant a garden, try a lawsuit, teach a class, cook a gourmet meal, prepare homemade ice cream, beat you at Scrabble, and solve a Rubik's Cube in under five minutes."

He lives in Oklahoma with his wife and children.

24340057R00085

Made in the USA
Middletown, DE
21 September 2015